The Gardener's Diary

The Gardener's Diary

A month-by-month guide
to what to do
in your garden and
greenhouse

Stanley
Whitehead

octopus

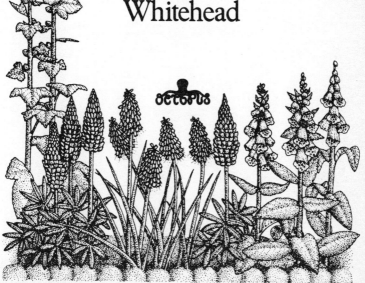

Stanley Whitehead is a very experienced gardener who has been writing and lecturing on the subject for several years. He edited the *Everyman's Encyclopaedia of Gardening* and has written numerous books as well as contributing frequently to magazines like *The Field* and *Popular Gardening*. Some of his recent books are *Basic Gardening*, *The Book of Garden Alpines*, *The Book of Flowering Shrubs and Trees* and *Garden Flowers*. He is also immersed in plant trials and other experiments in his own garden in North Lancashire.

First published in 1980 by
Octopus Books Limited
59 Grosvenor Street, London W1

This edition published in 1983 by
Octopus Books Limited
59 Grosvenor Street, London W1

© 1980 Hennerwood Publications Limited

ISBN 0 7064 2031 4

Made and printed in Great Britain by
Richard Clay (The Chaucer Press) Limited
Bungay, Suffolk

Illustrations by Liz Pepperell

Contents

Introduction

This book concentrates on the timing of gardening (rather than method or choice of plants), providing gardeners with general reminders of the seasonal tasks and detailed information of *when* to do *what*, and to *which* plants. Its aim is to help gardeners plan, create and sustain a place in which the plants they have chosen can thrive and provide maximum pleasure.

How to use this book
Each chapter is devoted to one month, and each can be read in isolation. Cross references have been kept to a minimum and jobs that are continuous over several months are given reminders in each month. It is important to note (and this is stressed throughout the book) that the monthly divisions are arbitrary and gardeners must act according to the situation and weather conditions prevailing (as described below) rather than to an exact date.

Within each chapter there are main sections on flowers, vegetables, fruit, the ornamental garden (subdivided into sections on hedges, paths, lawns, rock gardens, roses, shrubs, trees and water gardens) and gardening under glass – whether with simple frames or a greenhouse. At the beginning of the chapter there is a brief list of plants in flower or fruit that you may expect to see in this country during that month. These lists include the most common and popular flowering and fruiting plants and will enable the garden to be planted so it can be colourful and productive when you want it to be. Bear in mind that different varieties of plants can vary slightly in their fruiting and flowering times.

The index provides a comprehensive cross reference to both familiar and Latin plant names, and to the main activities covered in the book such as pruning, digging, propagating, fertilizing etc.

Thus the complete beginner, the newcomer to a particular aspect of gardening or the owner of a large and diverse garden, will find it easy to extract the desired information.

Any advice as to when to do something has necessarily to be qualified by the variations of situation and soil, and it therefore seems appropriate to examine these briefly.

Introduction

Situation

In the north of this country, the days begin to lengthen later in the year and to shorten sooner, resulting in lower temperatures than the south for most of the year. Consequently, northern gardens have a much curtailed active growing season, and will often be a couple of weeks behind at the beginning of the season or a couple of weeks ahead of the rest of the country at the end of the season. There is also a noticeable difference in climate between east and west. The rainfall is appreciably greater in the south and south-west than in the east and south-east. On the whole, the west coast is warmer than inland areas due to the influence of the Gulf Stream, which is notable even in northern Scotland.

The height of the garden above sea level is another important factor; the higher the garden, the colder it will be during late springs and early autumns. Cold air forms most readily on high ground and, being heavier than warm air, it flows downward over the surface (like water) replacing the rising warmer air to fill depressions and gather over valley floors, often carrying with it the threat of that dreaded late spring or early autumn frost.

Whatever part of the country the garden is in, its aspect to the sun will be of importance as there is a surprising difference between north and south facing parts of the garden, and between sunny and deeply shaded plots. Plants also vary in their tolerance of wind, which can not only be destructive but also intensifies the temperature and weather accompanying it. All these factors need to be considered when timing your gardening activities and, indeed, when choosing which plants to put in your garden.

Soil

The type of soil in your garden is of crucial importance as it will affect the choice of plants open to you, and its quality will affect their growth.

Sandy soils are loose, light to cultivate and unstable. Although they allow air and water to circulate freely, the valuable plant nutrients are easily lost in drainage and organic matter breaks down quickly – hence they are 'hungry' soils. They warm up quickly with the sun. *Clay soils* are dense, sticky and heavy to dig. Aeration is poor, drainage slow and they are cold soils. On the other hand, clay soils are inherently rich and can be made more friable with organic manuring and good drainage (see

November notes). *Loam soils* are defined as those with up to 50 per cent sand and no more than 20 per cent clay, mixed with fine sands and silt, and are as a result more rewarding to work. *Calcareous soils* overlie chalk or limestone formations and can be either light loams (quick draining and poor in plant nutrients) or heavy with clay. Their overriding characteristic is a high calcium content and alkaline soil reaction. *Peat soils* are very wet, strongly acid, tending to pack and shrink when cultivated and drained. Rhododendrons and azaleas thrive in them, but some liming and manuring will be necessary to grow a wider range of garden plants.

Drainage. Water and air occupy the spaces between the soil particles, and if there is too much water the roots and plants can drown; too little and they can dry out. Water drains through different soils at different speeds until it settles at a level called the water table. By digging a hole 2–3 ft deep you can study the behaviour of the water table and see how quickly it rises and falls after rain. If the top soil remains saturated for more than a few days then the chances are the drainage needs improving.

Soil acidity. The acid-alkaline balance of the soil is largely determined by the presence of lime, and garden plants are divided into those which are lime-tolerant (the majority, although in varying degrees) and those which are lime-haters (in particular the Heath family, azaleas, rhododendrons, Kalmia, Pieris etc.). If in doubt about the lime content, buy a simple testing kit (see February notes).

The key to improving any soil is to dig in humus-forming organic matter. It makes sandy soils more cohesive and moisture retentive, and clay soils more granular and porous; it provides the basis and the bank for plant nutrients; it helps restore any acid/alkaline imbalance, and it provides food and shelter for living organisms which transform mineral earth into a living soil structure wherein plant roots can grow strongly and healthily.

January

Some January plants in flower and vegetables in season

The Flower Garden	The Ornamental Garden	Vegetables in season
Christmas Rose	Heaths	Artichoke, Jerusalem
Crocus	Honeysuckle	Brussels sprouts
Iris Bakeriana	*Viburnum × burkwoodii,*	Cabbage
Snowdrop	*V. farreri,*	Leek
	V. tinus	Sprouting broccoli
	Winter Jasmine	
	Winter Sweet	

Although wintry conditions confine the gardener indoors, life in the garden goes on. Frost is a very good soil conditioner, particularly of clay. The clods and lumps expand as the action of freezing pushes the particles of soil apart. When the thaw comes they break down into smaller crumbs that are later easily raked to a fine surface tilth for sowing or planting. Ahead of frosts, use every hour of mild weather to dig, rotavate and turn over the soil, getting it done in time to allow the soil to reconsolidate before it is needed for sowing or planting.

Digging. This helps to aerate and drain the soil, to incorporate organic materials, to expose insect grubs to birds and weather, to improve rooting space for plants, and to give a pleasing surface finish. It is the best way to prepare vacant ground, which should be cleared of perennial weeds at the same time, with a cultivator or fork or by hand. Light, easily worked soils may need turning over only one spit deep, but heavy soils and clay benefit from double-digging in which the second spit is also

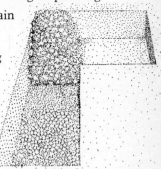

When double digging, fork manure into the second spit before filling in each trench

broken up. Heavy work like this is best dealt with in several short sessions rather than one exhausting burst, and made easier by using a good flat-tined digging fork or a spring-loaded spade.

☐ After the soil has been thoroughly prepared, less digging will be necessary in subsequent years. Instead, soil is mulched on the top, by spreading such organic materials as well-rotted manure, garden compost and leaf-mould in a layer several inches thick. This effectively keeps weeds down while nourishing the soil and helping it to retain moisture, but it is exacting of time and labour.

☐ In dry weather apply soil conditioners such as horticultural gypsum or calcified seaweed in granular form several days before digging. Never work on clay soils in wet weather: after compression the clay dries out so brick hard, it is impossible to work it to a crumbly texture.

☐ Avoid treading on lawns when they are brittle with frost, as

13

this bruises and damages the leaves of grass.

☐ Make up the list of seeds needed for the year and order them now. Send off for conifers, shrubs and evergreen trees for March–April planting.

☐ Now is the time to overhaul tools and power machinery: have petrol engines decarbonised and tuned, electric motors tested and plugs and cables examined for faults, and lawnmowers and cutting tools sharpened.

Wooden handles of spades, forks and trowels which have become rough should be rubbed down with sandpaper or steel wool, and dressed with linseed oil or a silicone wax polish. Steel blades can be restored to brightness by wetting and wiping with a rust-removing solution, and then oiling with machine oil.

☐ Treat garden woodwork – fences, posts, trellises and stakes – with a preservative harmless to plant life. Do not use creosote as the solution and its fumes are toxic to plants.

THE FLOWER GARDEN

In frosty weather, check that the soil has not started to lift up around autumn-planted stock, overwintering biennials (such as Canterbury bells (*Campanula medium*), foxgloves (*Digitalis purpurea*), honesty (*Lunaria annua*), stocks (*Matthiola incana*), mullein (*Verbascum thapsus*), wallflowers (*Cheiranthus cheiri*) and sweet williams (*Dianthus barbatus*) and cuttings in propagating beds. Firm it down without waiting for a thaw, when the soil will be too wet.

☐ In mild weather protect the growing tips of bulbs and corms from slugs and snails with ashes. Slug pellets of metaldehyde or methiocarb poison bait should be covered with polythene film to safeguard wildlife or pets.

☐ Make or remake flower beds and borders, working organic manure and slow-working fertilisers such as bone meal, hoof and horn meal and seaweed powder, into the top spit.

☐ When the ground is not hard with frost, herbaceous borders can be cleared of dead top growth and then top-dressed with well-rotted manure or compost distributed between plants. Cover crowns of such plants as delphiniums, peonies and

14

Michaelmas daisies with peat, forestry bark or old sawdust, so
that the new growth breaks through cleanly, uninfected by
botrytis disease (grey mould) which impairs flowering.

Top-dress lily of the valley (*Convallaria majalis*) with
manure or compost.

☐ Moss encroaching on beds and borders can be discouraged
with a sprinkling of nitro-chalk, immediately topped with
manure or compost.

Weed out roots of couch grass, dandelions, nettles, thistles
and perennial weeds. A 2-pronged weeding fork is most effective
in removing weed roots among plants, but if you prefer
chemical weedkillers, use a systemic weedkiller on new growth
as it shows.

THE VEGETABLE GARDEN

Crop rotation

Plan a crop rotation for outdoor vegetables to ensure that
vegetables of the same kind or family are not grown on the same
ground two years running. This minimises the risks of a build-
up in pests or disease, and uneven depletion of nutrients in the
soil. Exceptions are perennials such as globe artichokes, horse-
radish, rhubarb and perennial herbs such as mint and sage,
though even they need fresh ground occasionally. Onions can be
grown on the same ground for some years, provided the crop
remains healthy and profitable.

☐ For a three-year crop rotation, give onions a bed to
themselves, and divide the remaining ground into three for
these three groups of vegetables:

A   Peas, beans, leeks, celery, lettuces, spinach.
B   Cabbages, sprouts, kale, cauliflower, broccoli.
C   Potatoes and root vegetables

If there is not enough space for a separate onion bed,
include them with Group A. Potatoes take up a great deal of
land which many gardeners would prefer to devote to a larger
variety of crops. An answer to this problem for those who
would still like to enjoy the superior flavour of freshly picked
new potatoes of a variety not grown commercially, may be to
use grow-bags or barrels. It is essential to use only certified
disease-free seed potatoes from a reputable supplier.

Fertilisers. Vegetables in each of these groups have different but complementary needs, so prepare each plot annually to suit them. In the first year, apply manure or compost to plot 1 for Group A, fertilisers and lime to plot 2 for Group B, and fertilisers only to plot 3 for Group C. Each year move the groups of plants along to the next plot so that the rotation is:

	Year 1	Year 2	Year 3
Plot 1	Group A	Group B	Group C
Plot 2	Group B	Group C	Group A
Plot 3	Group C	Group A	Group B

In the fourth year start the sequence again. The beans and peas group require ground as rich as it can be made, while root crops should never be grown on freshly manured ground or they will be misshapen and the flavour impaired. Potatoes and other root crops must not be grown in freshly limed soil or they may develop scab. Brassicas (the cabbage group) do well on soil liberally manured for a previous crop, and their plot should be limed each year in the rotation as a precaution against club root disease.

☐ Keep organic fertilisers separate from lime in application, or they will react together to produce gaseous ammonia, which is harmful to both plant and animal life. Wait until two weeks after digging in fertilisers and then apply lime as a surface dressing to weather in. Chemical reactions are then slower and benign.

Sowing
Let soil temperature be your guide to first sowings. Buy a soil thermometer, and take the temperature at a depth of 5–7.5cm (2–3in.). Quick germination leads to stronger and more rapid growth, and seed takes longer to germinate in cold soils. Do not sow in recently frosted soil or after heavy rains, when seeds will rot, or, if they sprout, be vulnerable to fungus diseases. Late January is early enough in southern and mild areas. Wait 2 to 4 weeks in the north and on high ground. Make the first sowings in well-drained prepared soil in a warm sheltered position, but go by the soil temperature rather than the calendar.

☐ Raise the soil temperature to the required level 2 weeks in advance of sowing by covering it with cloches or a sheet of black polythene. When the soil temperature under the cloches reaches 10°C (50°F), try a sowing of longpod broad beans, set 5cm (2in.) deep, 15cm (6in.) apart in double or triple rows and give the seedlings the protection of cloches against sudden spells of hard weather.

☐ Shallots are well worth growing in the kitchen garden. Plant them now in humus-rich, well-drained soil. Set each one just below the surface, 15cm (6in.) apart, cover with soil and firm down. Put plastic netting on top to deter birds and cats until the leaves show green.

☐ Lift roots of rhubarb for forcing from plants three years old or more. Leave exposed to cold weather or frost for two weeks, then box or pot in moist soil or compost. Keep in a dark place, such as a cellar or shed, at 7–13°C (45–55°F) and keep moist.

☐ Lift mint roots to force a spring supply of leaves. Place in rich compost in shallow trays, well-firmed and moistened, and leave on a windowsill, warm porch or greenhouse at not less than 13°C (55°F).

☐ Set seed potatoes to sprout ('chit') as soon as available. Place each one eye-end up in shallow trays or pulp-board egg trays. Leave them to sprout where they will be in a steady temperature of 5–7°C (40–45°F). A cool greenhouse, frame or spare room will be suitable, and some light is necessary to encourage short, sturdy embryo shoots from each eye.

☐ Examine stored crops periodically for soundness. Keep carrots, beetroot, parsnips, swedes and turnips cool and slightly moist in sand; garlic and onions dry; and potatoes cool in complete darkness.

☐ Harvest leeks, lifting direct from the soil with a fork; Brussels sprouts, from the base of plants upwards; sprouting broccoli, taking the largest shoots first.

THE FRUIT GARDEN

Plant stone fruits – apricot, cherry, damson, plum, nectarine, and peach – before the end of the month, as they start into growth early in the year. Choose the first mild day when the soil is workable. Fruit trees need good drainage. If the soil is heavily acid (see February notes on soil testing), work ground limestone into the bottom of the planting hole and enrich the top spit with bone meal. Dress a light soil liberally with organic matter, hoof and horn meal and bone meal. Placing a flat stone or slate next to the stem of a tree encourages the roots to branch out sideways.

☐ Complete winter spraying of fruit trees early this month, before buds begin to swell. Give priority to stone fruits (see December notes).

Finish the winter pruning of apples and pears as soon as possible in mild weather (see December notes).

☐ Clear weeds and fallen leaves from around fruit trees and bushes before applying fertilisers and organic mulches.

☐ Cut out all the previous season's fruited canes of raspberries before weeding. Use a paraquat/diquat weedkiller to control green weeds, wetting the foliage on a dry, sunny mild day, but if the problem is couch or coarse grasses use a systemic weedkiller, taking care to confine it to weed leaves and stems.

Remove the tip growth of over-tall established raspberries, and cut out weak new shoots, leaving four to six shoots per stool or plant to be tied in to training wires for this year's fruiting.

☐ Clear strawberry beds of weeds, old, discoloured leaves, and unwanted runners, before top-dressing with sulphate of potash, and applying organic matter, such as compost or peat, liberally to the topsoil and mixing it in.

☐ Watch out for birds, especially finches, feeding on swelling fruit buds from the end of the month onwards. The best protection is a fruit-cage of metal or wood framework over which plastic netting can be draped and fastened. Otherwise, spray with a bird repellent, and repeat at intervals of 3 to 6 weeks. Scares and scarecrows need to be changed often to be effective; cotton threads strung from bush to bush may injure the birds.

THE ORNAMENTAL GARDEN

Hedges
Deciduous shrubs can be planted as hedges provided the soil is not frosted or waterlogged (see November notes). Rake out the tangled weeds from the bottoms of established hedges, to

disturb wintering insect grubs and pests and expose them to birds. To clear ivy, cut stems off at the base, let the aerial growth die before pulling it out, and paint the severed stumps with a strong sodium chlorate solution. Brambles and briars should be forked or dug out by the roots.

Trim and cut back overgrown deciduous hedges in fair weather between January and late March. Beech and hornbeam make regrowth well from pruning hard, that is, reducing hedges by up to half their height.

Paths

Making or repairing paths is a winter job. Paths intended for foot traffic only, such as paving stones, flags or elm-wood blocks can be laid directly on the soil. On heavy soils and in damp places, however, remove enough soil to allow for a 5–7.5cm (2–3in.) foundation of coarse sand, fine grit or ashes.

☐ For stepping-stone paths in grass, remove pieces of turf corresponding in size and shape to the stones, and enough soil for the stones to be set level with the soil surface.

☐ For much-used paths and driveways take out enough soil to allow for a 10–15cm (4–6in.) foundation of hard core of packed broken stone brickbats, rubble or clinker, topped with cinders or sand, under the flags or paving material.

☐ Gravel remains one of the cheapest and most easily maintained path surfaces. Spread it on a 7.5cm (3in.) layer of fine sand, and keep it weed-free with periodic applications of simazine.

☐ Treat hard paths made slippery with green algae, lichen and moss growth by thoroughly wetting the growth with a carbolic emulsion, or a 10 per cent solution of tar-oil wash. Choose a dry day for this job and treat algae, lichens, liverworts and mosses on brickwork, stonework and roofs at the same time.

Lawns

Lawns need little or no attention in frosty and dry cold weather. Snow is not harmful. A good trick is to scatter on the snow any steady-acting fertiliser (bone meal, powdered seaweed, or a slow-release nitrogenous fertiliser), which will be carried down as the snow melts.

Level uneven places in mild weather. Take the turf off in a

thin layer, remove or add soil underneath as necessary, and
replace the turf; firm it into place gently without beating or
heavy rolling.

Shallow depressions can be levelled by simply topping up
with a few handfuls of loamy soil to a depth of no more than
1cm (½in.) at a time. Let the grass grow through before adding
any more soil.

☐ Protect autumn-sown seedling lawns from cold drying winds
by covering with sheet polythene or slitted protective sheeting.

The Rock Garden

As alpine plants tend to flower early, use dry days to weed
thoroughly. Weeds which cannot be rooted out by hand or with
a small fork may be treated with chemical weedkiller as long as
care is taken to confine its application by using a paint-brush, or
long-spouted oil can. Wetting the crowns with a systemic
weedkiller has the advantage of controlling the weeds without
harming the soil. Oxalis, celandine, coarse couch grass,
buttercups, dandelions, and other persistent woody weeds can
be controlled in this way.

☐ Cover hairy- or woolly-leaved alpine plants with plastic caps
or rectangles of glass on wire clips to keep rain off and prevent
frost and snow lodging at the base of the stems, where it could
cause rotting.

Roses

If the weather is exceptionally mild, it may be possible to get
started with pruning. Opinions differ on the best time to prune.
For the technique of pruning, see February and March notes.

Shrubs

If new plants arrive from the nursery in cold or wet weather,
making it unwise to plant them, place them in their wrapping in
a shed, cold greenhouse or cellar, covered against any keen frost.
They may be left safely for up to three weeks. If bought with
bare roots, dig an outdoor V-shaped trench big enough to
accommodate the roots. Lay the plants in the trench at a 45°
angle. Cover the roots lightly, first with soil and then litter
(fallen leaves, twigs, straw). This is the process known as
'heeling-in' and the plants can be left until conditions are
favourable for planting.

A dressing of leaf-mould, peat or pulverised bark distributed over the roots of newly planted shrubs before filling up the planting hole with soil will check frost penetration and soil upheaval. Where soil does lift up tread it down again immediately.

☐ Give frost protection to shrubs of doubtful hardiness by surrounding them with a loose tent of polythene or sacking, or with bracken or straw, or with a pyramid of leafy evergreen branches.

☐ Heap and compost mixed fallen leaves for use in top-dressing lime-intolerant shrubs such as rhododendrons.

Trees
Young deciduous trees from the nursery with bare roots should be heeled-in (see Shrubs) if they arrive at a time when planting conditions are unfavourable. Evergreen and coniferous trees are best placed in a cool greenhouse or shed, even if their roots are in a ball of soil or container. Syringe the roots and foliage from time to time, until the bad weather passes and the soil is warmer and easier to work.

☐ Place temporary windbreaks of hurdles, pea-stick fences, or plastic sheeting on the windward side of conifers and evergreens planted the previous autumn. Cold biting winds can do a great deal of damage to newly planted shrubs and trees, lifting them out of the soil, breaking the roots and desiccating the foliage.

☐ Tie the branches of upright growing conifers such as cypresses and junipers together around the central stems to prevent heavy snow lodging on the boughs and breaking them.

The Water Garden
Keep the pond well filled. The water needs to be at least 45cm (18in.) deep if it is not to freeze solid. Aquatic plants could survive, but not fish.

☐ If your pond has fish in it, break gently any surface ice that forms with a sharp steel rod or drill, rather than a hammer. Fish are vulnerable to vibrations transmitted by water.

☐ Put one or two flat pieces of cork, a rubber tyre, toy or ball, or wooden boards to float in the water in winter and they will absorb the pressure as water freezes and expands. This prevents damage to pond walls.

If the pond should become iced over, do not let a carpet of snow lie on it for any length of time, as it will diminish the light reaching oxygenating plants. If they stop functioning, the oxygen level in the water will fall, and fish die.

Cover small shallow pools with a tent of sheet polythene or PVC when frost and hard weather are forecast.

☐ Remove dead stalks and leaves of marginal pond plants so that they do not fall into the pool and foul the water.

THE GARDEN UNDER GLASS

Glass, and its modern equivalents, transparent polythene and PVC, give plants protection from wind, rain and snow, while admitting sufficient quantities of the sun's life-giving light and heat rays. The success of gardening under glass depends on understanding the importance of providing fresh air, moisture and food to the plants, and tempering the warmth and light available to them in a closed environment.

The most vital influence on plant growth is available light. When days are short and the daylight weak, growth is slow and plants need less warmth, less watering, less ventilation and no feeding; but as the days lengthen, and the sun climbs higher, plants need more of all these things and therefore call for more attention.

The Cold Greenhouse

Only hardy plants can reasonably be grown in a structure without artificial heat during winter – young early-flowering shrubs such as camellias, dwarf brooms, ericas, forsythias, flowering currants, and *Daphne cneorum* in pots; hardy or near-hardy garden plants such as anemones, Brompton stocks, Christmas and Lenten roses, columbines, wallflowers and primulas, and alpines. Evergreen ferns are also useful. Sink pot plants to their rims in the greenhouse borders.

☐ Wash down all glass and internal surfaces with a mild fungicidal solution or disinfectant on a bright day. Open the ventilators to speed up drying and get rid of fumes.

☐ Change greenhouse border soil after two years' cropping, to prevent the soil becoming exhausted and diseases and pests taking hold. Replace the top spit entirely with good loam or a mixture of 3 parts by volume loam, 2 parts moist peat and 1 part coarse sand, all sterilised. Alternatively change over to ring culture or the grow-bag system for growing tomatoes and other summer crops.

☐ Prepare for ring culture by removing 15cm (6in.) of the soil from the staging or border; level the base and firm it down. Line with sheet polythene, evenly punched with small holes and fill up with an aggregate (gravel, weathered ashes and broken clinker). Place bottomless pots of rings filled with a balanced compost on the aggregate to hold the plants. A simpler alternative is to replace the top 5cm (2in.) of a bed with moist peat or pulverised forestry bark, on which to place the rings.

☐ Try to change the air on dull, damp days by opening the ventilators for half-an-hour or so at midday – a stagnant atmosphere encourages fungal rots, greening of the soil, and insect pests. Fan ventilation is a boon to counter such conditions.

☐ Make a sowing of dwarf peas ('Meteor', 'Feltham First') in large pots for an indoor crop in 12 weeks.
Sow lettuce ('Sutton's Fortune', 'May Queen' or 'Windermere') in boxes towards the end of the month, to be transplanted out of doors in April for spring cropping.
Sow dwarf French beans ('The Prince') in large pots or boxes to crop under glass.
Sow sweet peas, singly, in long peat or whalehide pots. Plants will be ready for setting out in March or April, without root disturbance.

☐ A useful accessory to the cold greenhouse is a heated propagating frame or unit, which by providing bottom heat (i.e. a warmed soil) makes it possible to make sowings early and get cuttings rooted quickly. Most available units work by soil-warming cables and need to be connected to an electricity supply.

The Cool Greenhouse
Heated to provide a minimum temperature of 7°C (45°F) on the coldest nights, a cool greenhouse increases the range of plants that can be grown in the cold weather months, but, most usefully, extends the growing season by making possible earlier

sowing of seeds and propagation by cutting as well as earlier cropping and harvesting. Heating may be by paraffin-oil, gas or electricity or by extension from the house central heating system. Keep a paraffin-oil-burning heater perfectly clean, and trim the wicks regularly. If you can smell the fumes, unburnt oil is vaporising and making the atmosphere toxic to plants. Good heaters are equipped with a flue to take the fumes outside to minimise this risk. Heating with gas, whether natural gas from the mains or a self-contained heater on bottled propane gas, is reasonably efficient and worth considering. For clean, easily managed, trouble-free and flexible heating use electricity. Mobile fan heaters, thermostatically controlled, distribute warmed air, and respond quickly to needs. Thermostatically controlled tubular heaters, consisting of tubes enclosing heating elements, running along the side walls of the greenhouse, are efficient and are the choice of most owners of small greenhouses.

□ Keep temperatures above 7°C (45°F) at night and above 10°C (50°F) during the day for plants such as perpetual flowering carnations, *Erica canaliculata*, *Gardenia jasminoides*, *Primula malacoides*, *P. obconica*, and *P. sinensis*, Indian azaleas (*Rhododendron simsii*), *Cyclamen persicum*, *Hippeastrum* hybrids, and half-hardy bulbous plants.

□ Make first sowings of hardy annual flowers when soil temperatures of 13–18°C (55–65°F) are possible. Seeds need a higher temperature in order to germinate; seedlings and young plants can grow on at slightly lower temperatures.

□ Make first sowings of cabbage ('Progress', 'May Express', 'Primo'), cauliflower ('All-The-Year-Round'), and lettuce ('Fortune', 'Windermere') at the end of the month, for transplanting outdoors in March or April.

Composts. Make up composts for seeds, seedlings and plants, and for greenhouse work to tested formulae, such as:

John Innes seed compost
2 parts by volume sterilised loam
1 part by volume sphagnum moss peat
1 part by volume coarse sand or small perlite pellets
plus per bushel (36.3 litres or 8 gallons)
40g (1½oz) superphosphate
20g (¾oz) ground chalk

John Innes potting compost No. 1
7 parts by volume sterilised loam
3 parts by volume sphagnum moss peat
2 parts by volume coarse sand or small perlite pellets
plus per bushel (36.3 litres or 8 gallons)
112g (4oz) John Innes base fertiliser
20g ($\frac{3}{4}$oz) ground chalk

For John Innes potting compost No. 2, used for potting on of most subjects and for bulbs and winter pot plants, follow the formula for No. 1, but double the quantities of fertiliser and ground chalk per bushel. For John Innes potting compost No. 3, used for so-called 'coarse feeders' such as tomatoes, final potting and rings in ring culture, triple the quantities. John Innes base fertiliser consists of 2 parts by weight hoof and horn, 2 parts superphosphate of lime and 1 part sulphate of potash.

Before mixing up the composts loam must be sifted and steam-sterilised. Although it is worth going to the trouble of mixing composts, not least because it is cheaper than buying them ready-prepared, the increasing difficulty in obtaining good loam has led to the use of loam-free or soil-less composts based on peat and sand or peat only. Several reliable proprietary brands are available, which should be used with fertilisers according to the manufacturer's instructions. Soil-less composts need more careful watering as peat once dried out is difficult to make water-absorbent again, and liquid feeding is needed during the flowering and maturing stages of plant growth.

Frames

Prepare frames by sponging both sides of the glass with a fungicidal solution and cleaning with algaecide if necessary.

Replace the soil in permanent brick-, stone-, or concrete-walled cold frames with fresh soil compost such as John Innes potting compost No. 2 to be used for early cropping of lettuce, radish, carrots, and spring onions.

Portable frames have the advantage that they can be moved to where they will be most practical, and can serve as large cloches. Used in conjunction with a soil- or air-warming kit, early salad vegetables may be grown and dwarf peas or beans started off. Pots or boxes of seedlings can be housed in the frame before being pricked out into pots, and autumn-taken cuttings from plants such as pelargoniums sheltered until successfully rooted and ready for potting on.

February

Some February plants in flower and vegetables in season

The Flower Garden
Aconite
Christmas Rose
Crocus
Cyclamen
Iris
Snowdrop

The Ornamental Garden
Clematis cirrhosa
Cornus mas (Dogwood)
Daphne mezereum
Garrya elliptica
Hamamelis mollis (witch hazel)
Heaths
Honeysuckle (*Lonicera fragentissima*)
Magnolia
Mahonia
Prunus conradinae, P. incisa
Saroccocca hookerana
Viburnum (see January)

Vegetables in season
Artichoke, Jerusalem
Brussels sprouts
Cabbage
Leek
Sprouting broccoli

Despite its reputation as a rainy month, February usually has more dry days than wet. From regions of high barometric pressure over Scandinavia blow north and east winds that are dry and chilling, though they also bring gripping frosts and snow. It is not until the end of February that there may be the occasional clear and sunny day, to be paid for in night frosts.

From February to early May, take into account the effects of latitude, site and soil condition, available light and especially air and ground temperatures on outdoor operations.

☐ Finish any deep digging or trenching of vacant soil as soon as weather permits. Break up topsoil well with a fork, and leave it rough for frost and thaw to break up the clods.

☐ Use moist and very well-rotted materials for organic manuring, whether farmyard manures, compost, peat, leaf-mould, forestry bark or weathered sawdust, so that they can be well worked into the soil. Unrotted manure slows down fertility by needing the attentions of bacteria which normally release nitrogen into the soil for plants.

☐ Condition heavy soils and clay with a calcified seaweed soil conditioner roughly raked in a few days before cultivating.

Lime. This is the month to apply lime as long as the soil has not just been organically manured. Leave an interval of at least two weeks between manuring and the application of lime, if lime is necessary for a particular crop or plant. Most garden plants thrive on soils that a slightly acid to neutral. The old-fashioned terms of 'sweet' for a soil with enough lime, and 'sour' for a soil needing lime, have little scientific accuracy. Too much lime can be as harmful as too little.

Lime improves the structure of heavy clay soils by promoting larger pore spaces, to the benefit of aeration and drainage. It also supplies calcium, a nutrient element essential to growing plants. Its key function, however, is to neutralise soil acidity so that mineral elements are made available as nutrients to plants.

Before liming, find out the acid–alkaline balance of your soil as expressed on the pH scale. This is a measurement of the hydrogen ion concentration, responsible for acidity, in the soil solution. On the pH scale, the number 7.0 indicates a neutral state; higher numbers indicate alkalinity, lower numbers acidity in geometrical progression; thus a soil of pH 5.0 is ten times more acid than one of 6.0. To check the balance of your soil, test it by using a proprietary soil-testing kit employing a colorimetric indicator solution. Take a small typical sample (or mixture of samples from different parts of a plot) from a depth of 5–10cm (2–4in.). The chart shows how to use the colour results to obtain the pH scale reading.

The majority of garden plants make optimum growth in soils of pH 6.4 to 6.8. No lime is necessary on soils of a higher pH value. Many shrubs, trees, flowering plants, lawn grasses, crops such as cucumbers, marrows, potatoes and tomatoes, and fruits such as raspberries, strawberries and blackberries prefer soils of marked though moderate acidity. Members of the Heath or *Ericaceae* family usually need a strongly acid soil, without free lime in it.

If you need to add some form of lime, the amount required will depend on (a) the level of pH most helpful to the crop or plants to be grown; (b) the nature of the soil; and (c) the kind of liming material applied.

Use hydrated or slaked lime in finely powdered form for the quickest reaction. Two other liming materials most useful for gardens are ground chalk and ground limestone. As lime in these forms does not burn plants it can be applied at any time of year, but works most effectively into the soil during a rainy period.

They are all three forms of natural deposits of calcium carbonate, suitable for use on all soils at any season, but ground chalk and limestone are less soluble than hydrated lime, and best applied ahead of the growing season in winter. For general garden use, they should be in finely ground condition. Chalk, as a slightly softer and more moisture-absorbent material than limestone, is most useful on acid sands and light soils. Ground limestone is good for all soils, particularly acid clays. As ground chalk and limestone act more slowly than hydrated lime, the amounts used should be increased by about a third to bring about the same change in pH.

Apply lime more sparingly on light and open textured soils than on heavy or clayey soils where acidity is corrected more quickly.

Test every third year for pH value and possible need of lime. Lime is lost from soils both in chemical reactions and by leaching or drainage. When bastard-trenching previously unworked ground on deep heavy clay soils, apply limestone grit

A GUIDE TO THE pH VALUES OF SOILS

pH value of soil	General rating	Colour reaction	Effect on the availability of plant nutrients in the soil	Effect on plants and their growth
7.7 and higher	very strongly alkaline	green-blue	rarely encountered in gardens; reduced availability of all mineral elements	strong chlorosis (yellowing of the leaves), sparse stunted growth
7.6–7.3	strongly alkaline	olive green	availability of trace elements (phosphorus potassium, iron, manganese, boron, and sodium reduced.	stunted, thin growth; tendency to chlorosis in green-leaved plants; reduced flowering. Tolerated best by plants native to chalk, and some shrubs.
7.2–7.0	neutral	yellow green	some reduction in the availability of trace elements to some plants.	a tendency to chlorosis in green-leaved plants, especially those preferring acid soils. Much depends upon the humus and organic content. Most plants do well with liberal organic manuring.
6.8–6.4	slight to moderate acidity	yellow	maximum availability of all mineral nutrient elements to plants.	optimum reaction for healthy growth in most ornamental garden plants, flowers, fruit and food crops, excepting the lime-intolerant.
6.3–5.5	moderate to strong acidity	orange	declining availability of phosphates, and tendency to diminishing calcium, magnesium and potassium by leaching.	acceptable to lawn grasses, the majority of shrubs, trees and flowering plants; to potatoes, tomatoes, cucumbers, marrows, blackberries, raspberries and strawberries.
5.4–4.5	strong to very strong acidity	red	very poor availability of phosphorus, deficiency in calcium and magnesium. Most mineral nutrients tend to be more soluble and leached.	poor top-growth, tendency to white marginal leaf scorch and distortion, stunted and poorly formed root system. Excellent, however, for lime-intolerant members of the *Ericaceae* family.

to the second spit, where it is effective for some years.

As a general guide, lime should be applied at the rate of about 225g/m² (8oz per sq. yd) where necessary, but applications vary according to soil type and structure.

THE FLOWER GARDEN

Delay sowings and lifting of plants for division to the end of the month or leave until March in northern England and Scotland, until the light strengthens and temperatures begin to rise. This means being two to four weeks behind gardeners in the south. Take into account the reaction of native plants to climatic conditions; the soil temperature and how quickly it begins to rise, which will depend on the aspect and texture, height above sea level, and exposure to the sun's warmth.

☐ Place glass or plastic cloches or hand-lights over early-flowering bulbs and corms and hellebores likely to be injured by adverse weather. Scatter a thin mulch of ashes, coarse sand or grit around the stems to keep slugs at bay.

☐ Take advantage of sunny mild days to lift and move deciduous shrubs, if necessary, herbaceous plants and ferns to new quarters in the garden; lift with plenty of soil clinging to the roots and do not allow them to dry out before replanting.

☐ Plant lily of the valley (*Convallaria majalis*) crowns or pips with tips just below the soil surface. Choose a site in partial shade with well-drained soil enriched with leaf-mould or well-rotted organic matter. They take a year to become established. The variety 'Fortin's Giant' gives larger, longer-stalked flowers a fortnight later than the type; 'Rosea' has rose-pink-tinted, strongly scented flowers and is less vigorous.

☐ Plant corm-like tubers of *Anemone coronaria* of the St Brigid and De Caen strains, and *A. × fulgens* in moist rich loam 5cm (2in.) deep, to give early summer bloom, a little later than the October-planted tubers.

☐ Plant the claw-like roots of the half-hardy *Ranunculus asiaticus* in the handsome colourful flowering forms of the Persian, turban and peony-flowered varieties in the last week of the month. They need a sunny sheltered site and good loam soil and will flower in June.

☐ Take advantage of the first dry days to weed, refirm the roots, and rake in a light dressing of a nitrogenous fertiliser such as dried blood or hoof and horn meal to bedded-out stocks and wallflowers.

Dividing snowdrops

☐ As soon as the flowers drop, lift clumps of snowdrops that have become overcrowded, divide and replant immediately, without exposing the roots to dehydration by air. Space large bulbs 10cm (4in.) apart. If replanted with care, the plants make vigorous leaf growth and are one of the few bulbous plants successfully propagated in this way.

☐ Check primroses, polyanthus, and autumn-planted pansies and violas for slug damage in mild weather. Slug pellets are effective but harmful to wildlife and pets; an alternative is to water in a solution of metaldehyde.

☐ Give a top-dressing of fine bone meal and well-rotted manure or compost to crown imperials (*Fritillaria imperialis*) early this month. A well-drained site is essential, and it is advisable to plant the bulbs on their sides to prevent water collecting in the depression on the top. The lemon-yellow variety 'Lutea' is outstanding and looks magnificent in full spring sunshine.

☐ Lift and divide hardy herbaceous border plants while still dormant, removing the roots of invading weeds such as couch grass, horsetails and bindweed before replanting.

THE VEGETABLE GARDEN

Be guided in making early sowings by soil temperature: wait until it reaches at least 10°C (50°F); soil porosity: light, open sandy soils may be sown well before heavy, moist ones; weather: the surface soil should be beginning to dry out. When in doubt, delay as there is nothing to be gained in premature sowings which will be slow or fail to germinate.

Sow main crops of broad beans, longpod or Windsor varieties, 5cm (2in.) deep, 15–23cm (6–9in.) apart, staggered in double or triple rows, from the middle of the month in soil to which sulphate of potash has been added at the rate of 16g/m² (½oz per sq. yd).

Seeds of first early peas ('Feltham First', 'Kelvedon Wonder', and 'Hurst Beagle') may be sown in mild southern gardens from mid-February, later elsewhere, in well-drained soil manured the previous autumn.

Sow parsnips in deep permeable soil for good unforked roots. On heavy ground, make holes 30–45cm (12–18in.) deep, 20cm (8in.) apart, with a dibber, fill with sand or sandy loam, and sow each with two seeds 1cm (½in.) deep. Remove the weaker seedling later.

Choose the sunniest, warm spot for garlic; a free-draining loam, enriched with an organic fertiliser is best, and plant bulb segments (cloves) upright, 1cm (½in.) deep, 30cm (12in.) apart, in the first half of February. Garlic needs ample spring and early summer sun.

Make first sowings of summer spinach ('Monarch Long Standing') in mid to late February on soil well-manured for a previous crop.

Given a warm, sheltered position, and rich light loam, February sowings of lettuces 'Little Gem' and 'Winter Density' should be rewarding. Sow seeds 5mm (¼in.) deep, in rows 30cm (12in.) apart, and thin the seedlings to 20cm (8in.).

☐ Dress overwintered spring cabbage with a quick-acting nitrogenous fertiliser (dried blood or nitro-chalk) as soon as temperatures begin to rise at the end of the month.

☐ Prepare V-shaped drills, 30–38cm (12–15in.) deep for early potatoes. Where small black soil-frequenting slugs are a nuisance, limit the use of organic manures. A well-cultivated plot should be chosen and metaldehyde bait laid down.

☐ Prepare ground for asparagus by deep digging, removing every scrap of perennial weed roots, and organic manuring very liberally, in readiness for April planting (see April notes).

THE FRUIT GARDEN

Resolve not to let bush fruits or fruit trees carry any crop in their first year. Prune blackcurrant bushes hard to the second bud on shoots above soil level. Cut back the canes of newly planted raspberries to about 15cm (6in.) above ground level. Prune newly planted gooseberry, red and white currant bushes by cutting shoots to outward facing buds, about 7.5cm (3in.) from their base.

☐ Prune the fruited canes of established autumn fruiting raspberries such as 'November Abundance', 'Hailsham' and 'Zeva' to within 15cm (6in.) of the ground.

☐ Prevent the fungus responsible for leaf curl on outdoor nectarines and peaches by spraying with a lime-sulphur, copper or benomyl fungicide when the buds are about to open in mid to late February.

☐ Be ready to protect early flowering nectarines, peaches, cherries, and plums on walls with a draping of sheet polythene, netting or sacking on nights when radiation frosts are forecast.

☐ Prevent rabbit damage to fruit trees by wrapping the main stems in a bite-resistant plastic collar, or a sleeve of fine-mesh netting.

THE ORNAMENTAL GARDEN

Hedges
Plant hedges of flowering plums early this month. A good choice is the crimson-leafed, spring-flowering *Prunus × cistena*, with white flowers, or *P. cerasifera* 'Atropurpurea', syn. 'Pissardii' and its form 'Nigra', which are purple-leafed, with pink flowers in spring. They need an ordinary well-drained soil, to which lime should be added, if acid.

☐ Finish clearing hedge bottoms of dead grass and plant debris, so that birds can forage for lurking insects and their grubs.

Paths

Clear paths of cinder, brick rubble and dust; clear gravel of all weed top growth with the hoe; rake and then apply a residual weedkiller containing simazine to last for the rest of the year.

Using a brush, or by sprinkler bar, apply a concentrated solution of a total weedkiller to weeds between paving stones or flags, but not near lawns or garden plants. For moss and green algae growth see January notes.

Lawns

Invest in a turf-aerating tool if you want to maintain a top quality lawn; a simple fork with tines or prongs will do for small lawns, but a rotary manual or power-driven tool is needed to cope with large areas. For lawns on free-draining soils, spiking or slitting tines are sufficient; on heavy soils and turf subject to much compaction hollow tubular tines which take out small cores of soil are invaluable. Apart from aerating turf at the roots and refreshing root growth, spiking and slitting prepare the way for top dressings and fertiliser dressings to enter the soil and ameliorate growing conditions.

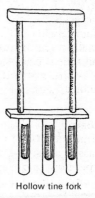

Hollow tine fork

☐ Top-dress lawns on heavy soils with coarse sand, fine grit, perlite or vermiculite, plus a soil conditioner and brush in, after aeration treatment. On light soils, use sifted lawn peat, or, at a pinch, the contents of spent grow-bags.

☐ Complete laying of new turf by the end of the month, particularly on light soils, so that it has time to make roots and integrate with the soil before the dry spells of spring occur (see November for practical techniques).

☐ Worm casts strewn on the lawn look untidy, but bear in mind that the casts are enriched fertile soil and only a few earthworm species make them. When the casts are drying out and friable, scatter them over the grass with a long whippy cane or the back of a springbok rake as a top-dressing. To deal with excessive worms use an expellent and sweep up the surfacing worms, or apply derris dust, bulked with sand, as a safe vermicide. This still leaves a population of other earthworm species naturally beneficial to the soil.

The Rock Garden
The construction of a new rock garden or terrace in the open could get underway now. Avoid draughty, shady and low-lying sites. For inspiration study rock gardens at shows and in gardens open to the public, or rock outcrops occurring naturally in hilly country. If possible choose a site with a southerly aspect on an east-to-west axis. If the only site available faces north or is somewhat shaded, plants will need to be selected very carefully. Above all ensure good drainage; this is the crucial factor in successfully growing plants whose native habitat is a rocky mountainside. Put a deep drainage layer of brick, rubble or small stones at the bottom of terraces and pockets. Fill up with soil that is completely free of perennial weeds, and which is up to a third grit and gravel. Enrich with leaf-mould and small quantities of slow-acting organic fertilisers only.

Roses
Prune new bush roses of the hybrid tea (HT) type, now to be classed as large-flowered roses, and the floribunda or polyantha type, now to be classed as cluster-flowered roses, straight after planting this month and next. See that the graft union is set just below the soil surface, firm the roots well, and cut all top shoots back to outward-pointing buds about 15cm (6in.) from the base.

☐ See that newly planted standard roses are securely staked, and prune shoots when the weather turns mild at the end of the month or in March, reducing shoots to within three buds or eyes of their base at the graft-union. Do not cut into the older wood.

☐ Prune newly planted climbing hybrid tea and floribunda roses by shortening young shoots only by up to a third of their length, and then arch and tie in the stems in a fan-shape or horizontally. Avoid pruning the variety 'Mermaid' and the repeat-flowering climbers such as 'Autumn Sunlight', 'Casino', 'Compassion', 'Coral Dawn', 'Danse du Feu', 'Golden Showers', 'Schoolgirl', 'Swan Lake', and 'New Dawn', in their first year.

☐ Newly planted shrub roses need no pruning except the removal of dead or broken shoots, or weak growth.

☐ Well-planted in prepared ground, organically manured and limed to pH 6.5, new roses are best left to establish themselves without stimulating fertilisers during their first year. They form good root systems and thereafter live longer.

☐ Apply a well-balanced fertiliser, specially formulated for roses, or a top-dressing of well-rotted organic manure to established specimens in late February or early March, lightly forked into the rooting area of the roses.

Shrubs

Spray ornamental shrubs and trees of the *Prunus* genus such as flowering almonds, cherries, peaches and plums with a lime-sulphur, copper or benomyl fungicide to control leaf curl, at the same time as the related stone fruits are treated (see note in The Fruit Garden).

☐ When their planting stations are not ready, plant young deciduous shrubs or trees in large compressed peat, whalehide or black polythene pots in good compost, and stand in a wind-sheltered place, where they can be checked periodically and watered in dry weather. They can be kept in this way for several weeks and planted out when convenient. Make planting holes large enough to receive them, and put the plants in the holes still in their containers, which may be slit through without disturbance to the roots. Spread the roots out well, fill up the hole and settle it down with added soil. To hold back for shorter periods, plant in wooden bins, boxes or troughs in well-moistened peat or compost, or heel them in (see January notes).

☐ For deciduous herbaceous ground cover between and under shrubs and trees, plant *Brunnera macrophylla*, *Geranium nodosum*, *Hosta* species and varieties, *Omphalodes cappadocica*, *Pulmonaria angustifolia*, *P. officinalis*, and ferns such as *Dryopteris carthusiana*, *Matteuccia struthiopteris* and *Thelypteris phegopteris*.

☐ On shallow soils, chalk, heavy clay, made-up soil or tips, or soil that has been under buildings for years, plant shrubs and trees with roots at surface level. Before planting, break up the soil itself well, working in well-rotted manure or compost or peat, then plant with the roots spread out on top and good loam soil mounded over them. Take care not to let the roots come into contact with fresh manure. Stake securely.

Trees

Plant deciduous trees as soon as conditions permit, especially those which flower or leaf early in spring.

Plant trees of larger size and semi-maturity with extra care. If bought in with bare roots, place in a slurry or thin cream of water, loam soil and rotted manure overnight or for a day or two. Plant in a moist soil that has been well worked with organic compost, peat or similar material. Firm the roots in well. Bare, tough woody roots can be shortened, but preserve all the fibrous root you can. If bought with roots in soil in a container, place the tree in its planting station before removing the outer container; then fill in with a good topsoil or loam mixed with well-rotted organic matter and a good lacing of bone meal 30cm (12in.) all round. The surrounding soil must be fertile to entice the roots to grow out of the container ball. Stake the tree securely and water well in dry weather. Large specimens make an instant effect, but may not put on more growth for a year or more, until the root system expands.

Walls

Prune overgrown winter-flowering Jasmine, *Jasminum nudiflorum*, towards the end of the month if it has finished flowering. Unfasten from its supports and thin out the older stems, cutting back to just above a good new lateral shoot low down, or remove oldest stems entirely. Trim back the flowered shoots to within a bud or two of their base, and then re-position remaining shoots to the space available. Top-dress the roots with an organic mulch and fertiliser. This plant often propagates itself by rooting at the ends of shoots reaching the soil, and such shoots can be severed and planted out – try one draping a bank or terrace wall from the top.

The Water Garden

Making a new garden pond. Choose a position where a pond will receive good light, either morning or afternoon and evening sun. Shade at midday, however, from adjacent garden features such as trees, shrubs or hedges is helpful. Place out of the reach of tree roots and heavy, leaf-shedding branches. Shape depends on the style of the garden – formal, informal or natural – and on personal preferences. Size will decide the kind and number of plants that can be grown. An area of at least 75cm (2ft 6in.) deep is needed for a pool that is stocked with fish all year round.

Excavate 10–15cm (4–6in.) more all round than the finished dimensions for a concrete-lined pond, which will give you the most permanent structure and can be fitted with a drainage outlet. Seal the inner surface by treating with a proprietary sealant before filling and planting. Prefabricated pools in fibreglass or plastic need only an excavation into which they fit firmly; level soil irregularities with sand and remove all stones and other sharp objects.

When making ponds by lining excavations with waterproof plastic sheeting, lay the lining on a base of at least 5cm (2in.) of sand. Slope the walls outward to take the lining evenly, overlapping it at the top for anchorage with large stones or a flagged surround. Heavy sheet ploythene (500g (1lb) has a life of up to seven years before becoming brittle; butyl rubber lasts longer; but both are subject to damage from sharp tools.

☐ In established ponds watch out for duckweed (*Lemna minor*), the tiny floating aquatic plant which multiplies rapidly as daylight increases. In strict moderation it is helpful, but without resident waterfowl to eat it, keep it in check by drawing netting or a sheet of paper over it and removing with the weed clinging to it.

THE GARDEN UNDER GLASS

The longer days of February herald the propagation in earnest of plants from seeds.

☐ Use cloches for early outdoor cropping and raising of plants. Originally bell-like glass covers with a knob on top, modern cloches are tented or box-like structures of glass or translucent plastic material placed end-to-end in rows. Glass gives a firmer structure and promotes a slightly warmer interior atmosphere, though it is more easily broken. Both glass and plastic give plants shelter from wind and weather and transmit light and heat rays from the sun to provide slightly higher temperatures than those prevailing outside, creating a micro-climate favourable to seed germination and growth.

Place cloches in position over organically enriched good moist soil, with a compound fertiliser dressing raked in, a few days before sowing, to allow the soil to warm up.

☐ Under low cloches sow beetroot ('Boltardy'), early carrots ('Amsterdam Forcing', 'Nantes'), radish ('Carter's Sixteen Days', 'Cherry Belle'), lettuce ('Little Gem', 'Winter Density') and salad onion ('White Lisbon'). Under tall or barn cloches, sow early dwarf peas ('Feltham First', 'Early Onward' or 'Progress No. 9') and broad bean ('Sutton's Dwarf'), for early crops.

☐ Clean the lights of cold frames; replace the soil if it has been cropped for more than two years and sow early crops as described above for cloches.

☐ In a heated frame, propagator, or greenhouse border with soil-heating cables giving bottom heat of 10–13°C (50–55°F), make sowings of Brussels sprout F_1 'King Arthur', cabbage 'Primo', celery ('Giant White', 'Giant Pink', 'Golden Self-blanching'), leek ('Lyon', 'Musselburgh'), lettuce ('Unrivalled', 'Windermere') and cauliflower ('All the Year Round') for transplanting outside in May.

Greenhouse Gardening
Raise plants from seeds in standard compost for uniform success. There are several methods of seed propagation. The time-tested technique is to sow seeds in shallow wooden trays, $36 \times 20 \times 5$cm ($14 \times 8 \times 2$in.), half-trays or seed pans, but plastic trays of similar size are now often preferred. Alternatively, small pots of peat/wood fibre in blocks or strips may be used, which allow seedlings to grow without suffering the setback of being pricked out. When only small quantities of seedlings and plants are required, seeds may be sown in compartmented plastic trays, in peat discs, or in small, lightly compressed blocks of seed compost, to grow on singly and be transplanted without any root disturbance.

Place the chosen seed containers, filled with compost well moistened with tepid water, in the greenhouse some hours before sowing. Sow seeds shallowly, at about twice their diameter, and evenly spaced apart. Fine seeds need no more than pressing into the surface. Cover trays and pans with a sheet of glass or thick plastic, and brown paper. Turn the glass or plastic over daily, wiping it free of moisture. Remove the paper as soon as a few green shoots show. Give good light, but not direct sun, placing seedlings near to the source of light or the glass roof of the greenhouse to induce sturdiness as growth is made. Water to keep compost moist, not sodden, with a fine spray. Remove the glass covering when seedlings reach it. Seedlings in square blocks can be placed together in trays until transplanted.

☐ Germination may be speeded up by providing bottom heat in a heated propagating unit or frame or on a heated base plate.

Seeds of hardy annuals such as alyssum, anchusa, *Bartonia aurea*, calendula, coreopsis, mignonette, nasturtium, *Nicandra physaloides* and half-hardy annuals such as acroclinium, ageratum, alonsoa, arctotis, aster, gerbera, and *Phlox drummondii* need bottom heat of 10–15.5°C (50–60°F).

Give seeds of most half-hardy annuals and half-hardy perennials grown as annuals bottom heat of 15.5–21°C (60–70°F); while a few more tender plants such as begonias, petunias, fuchsias and pelargoniums grown for outdoor summer bedding, need bottom heat of 21–25°C (70–78°F).

Reduce the air temperature by 2 to 3°C (5°F) for all plants once germination has occurred.

The Cold Greenhouse
For flowers and foliage, grow young plants of *Abutilon megapotamicum*, varieties of *Camellia japonica*, *C. sasanqua,* and *C. × williamsii, Daphne odora*, varieties of *Erica herbacea* and *E. erigena, Fatsia japonica, Hamamelis × intermedia* varieties, *Viburnum × bodnantense* and *V. tinus* 'Eve Price', in pots or troughs, which can be planted outdoors in April–June. A wide range of bulbs and corms can be flowered in pots, especially species of crocus, *Galanthus* (snowdrop) and iris, with varieties of *Cyclamen coum* flourishing in deep pans.

The Cool Greenhouse
All the above plants can be enjoyed, as long as they are shaded from excessive sun and rapid rises in temperature. Mimosa (*Acacia dealbata*), varieties of *Epacris impressa* and the brightly berried *Solanum capsicastrum* can be added.

☐ Set dahlia tubers in pots or boxes, in moist peat, pulverised bark, sand, perlite or vermiculite and start into growth to provide cuttings for propagation, in temperatures of about 10°C (50°F). Gently prise off shoots at the base when they have made their first new leaves, and insert them singly in small pots or blocks of John Innes No. 1 compost on an equivalent soil-less compost to grow on.

☐ Plant up tuberous begonias in the same way to provide shoots which can be taken as cuttings; or in deep pots of potting compost to grow on undisturbed and flower in early summer.

☐ Divide the fleshy rhizomes of *Canna* species (Indian shot) into suitably sized pieces and plant them in moist peat, in beds or boxes at 15.5°C (60°F). Transfer them to a richer compost when roots have formed and growth shows, in single 12-cm (4½-in.) pots, to grow on.

☐ Pinch out the growing tips of autumn-rooted zonal pelargoniums and pot into small pots. Increase water gradually, and maintain a temperature of not less than 10°C (50°F).

☐ Cross-pollinate flowers of apricot, nectarine and peach trees under glass when fully open, transferring pollen on a camel-hair brush or rabbit's tail from one flower to another. Do this in the morning or evening, rather than in full sun.

☐ Make sowings of capsicum (sweet peppers), cayenne or chilli peppers, cucumber, egg plant (aubergine), melon and tomato seeds, for summer-cropping under glass. Supply bottom heat of 20°C (68°F). Pot them off singly into balanced composts at the early seedling stage, when the first true leaves have appeared.

Berberis - purple ones.(deciduous ones).

Remove unwanted branches, or damaged ones if necessary.

Sumach - cut stems to 1 foot above ground.

March

Some March plants in flower and vegetables in season

The Flower Garden

Aconite
Aubrieta
Bergenia
Christmas Rose
Crocus
Cyclamen
Daffodil
Erythronium
  (dog's tooth
  violet)
Grape hyacinth
Hyacinth
Heliotrope
Hepatica
Iris
Marsh marigold
Primula
*Pulsatilla
  vulgaris*
  (Pasque flower)
Saxifraga
Scilla
*Tulipa
  kaufmanniana*

The Ornamental Garden

Chaenomeles
  (flowering
  quince,
  japonica)
Cornus mas
  (Dogwood)
Corylopsis
*Daphne
  mezereum*
Forsythia
Hamamelis
  (witch hazel)
Heaths
Magnolia
Mahonia
Parrotia
Prunus (see
  February)
Ribes (flowering
  currant)
*Sorbus
  megalocarpa*
Willow (*Salix
  caprasa, S.
  gracillistyla, S.
  sachalinensis*)

Vegetables in season

Artichoke,
  Jerusalem
Brussels sprouts
Leek
Spinach
Sprouting
  broccoli

March can be very wintry with frost, ice and snow, and it is as well to be prepared especially when the early part of the month is mild. There are periods of wind that can be drying, but they usually lack the force of winter gales, and can be punctuated by remarkably quiet spells, when the sun asserts itself more and more.

It is a busy month for the gardener, first in making final preparations for the growing season, and secondly in planting and sowing out of doors. At this stage of the year the state of the soil and the climatic conditions must decide when and what can be done, not the calendar.

Prepare for sowing. Break down previously rough-dug soil after frost or rain as soon as the surface begins to dry, first forking, then raking and finally firming to a fine crumbly texture or tilth. On heavy or clay soils, choose the right moment to work – when clods break easily to a blow from the back of a fork, and before they dry brick hard.

March is too late for deep digging of clay soils. Any cultivations carried out on ground neglected over the winter should be confined to the top few inches of soil. Work in well-decomposed, not fresh, organic compost or manure, or one of the dehydrated concentrated manures with a fork and rake. Tread loose soil firm by laying a board or plank down and walking over it. Apply a compound fertiliser, then rake and cross-rake till the soil is fine and level.

☐ If you are making a new garden in March, concentrate on getting the soil weed-free, establishing good drainage, enriching it with humus-forming organic materials, and checking its acid–alkaline balance. Flower beds and borders can be sown with annuals or planted up with bedding plants for first year colour and effect. Note their performance for clues to the potentials of your garden. Gather their remains, when spent, for compost. Areas intended for fruit, shrubs, vegetables, or lawns should be heavily manured and given over to potatoes, intercropped with beans and peas, to give a friable soil for autumn planting.

☐ Delay early sowings until the soil is warm enough, that is, at least 13°C (55°F). If in doubt check with a soil thermometer, in the evening or early morning, at 7.5cm (3in.) deep. Light porous sandy soils heat up more quickly than heavy, moisture-retentive clays, but they also cool down more rapidly.

A week or ten days before sowing or planting, dress seed beds and planting stations with a compound base fertiliser, balanced to provide a range of nutrients.

Sowing. The more readily and vigorously seeds germinate, the better plants they make. To germinate quickly they need air, moisture and, most critical, warmth. To supply these needs the soil should be porous, but moist, and the seeds should not be sown so shallowly that they dry out, nor so deeply that they are oxygen-starved.

☐ Make seed-drills with the back of a rake or a triangular hoe, and seed trenches with a Dutch hoe. Although one hundred per cent germination is very unlikely, space seeds well to minimise the spreading of disease and to simplify thinning of seedlings. As a guide, sow seeds at two to three times their width or diameter, a little more deeply in light, sandy or gravelly soils; a little nearer the surface in moist heavy clays.

☐ In light soils that dry out quickly, cover the seeds with moist peat, leaf mould or old compost rubbed through a fine sieve; this will also prevent crusting-over after rain which checks soil aeration. On heavy, dense soils that are easily saturated, cover with sharp sand, perlite or vermiculite. On loamy, well-crumbled soils, cover with topsoil, lightly tamped down.

☐ Dress seeds by shaking them up with a little fungicidal/insecticidal powder before sowing to avoid losses from soil-borne infections such as damping-off and foot-rots, and insect pestsas flea beetles, weevils and wireworms. A 50/50 combination of a thiram or captan fungicide and a derris or BHC insecticide in powder form can be made up.

Fertilisers. Use fertilisers according to the manufacturers' instructions; their purpose is to provide plants with essential nutrients for growth. They are concentrated and may be of inorganic (chemical) or organic (plant or animal) origin. Too much at any one time can harm both soils and plants.

☐ Plants obtain at least 12 essential mineral nutrient elements from the soil. Seven of these are needed in relatively large quantities, namely nitrogen, phosphorus, calcium, magnesium, potassium, sulphur and iron; the five minor or trace elements needed in very small quantities are manganese, boron, copper, zinc and molybdenum. All are vital to healthy plant growth.

The natural sources of these elements are the mineral rock particles, organic matter, air and water of which soils are formed. They are made available to plant roots by complex physical, chemical and biological reactions between soil particles and organisms such as soil bacteria in the form of soluble chemical salts in a dilute soil solution. What plants do not take up may be stored in the soil or lost by leaching and drainage. Under cultivation, soils lose nutrient salts more quickly than they can be replaced naturally.

☐ Soil fertility is based on the presence of actively decomposing, humus-forming organic matter within it. Fertilisers are neither a substitute for nor an alternative to organic manuring, but are best regarded as complementary and subordinate. They are designed to supply the nutrient elements most subject to loss and/or deficiency in soils – nitrogen, phosphorus and potash (potassium). Sulphur is rarely deficient and occurs as a second element in many ingredients. Calcium is supplied, when needed, by liming. The need for magnesium and iron arises only in special circumstances and with certain crops and plants.

☐ A deficiency in a minor element can be as detrimental to plant growth as one in a major nutrient. It can be avoided by adding special mixtures of the minor elements in the form of frits (fuses glass-like particles) to base fertilisers used on poor deficient soils. Trace elements are also available in special liquid feeds for use in the growing season (see July notes).
Rate fertilisers according to
1. their nutrient content, usually expressed in percentages of nitrogen (N), phosphorus (P or P_2O_5 (phosphoric acid)), and potassium (K or K_2O (potassium oxide)), which determines their effect on plant growth;
2. whether they are inorganic (which means chemical, synthetic or from natural mineral deposits), or organic, derived from plant or animal remains;
3. speed of action, which means their solubility and how quickly they provide nutrients to plant roots;
4. end-reaction, acid or alkaline, which influences their effect upon the pH of a soil, and suitability for certain soils and plants.
All fertilisers contain other elements as well as those needed as plant nutrients, and sometimes this is important.

GARDEN FERTILISERS

NITROGEN is needed for all plant growth functions, for robust stem and leaf growth and rich green colour

Sources	Other nutrients present	When to use	Remarks
Inorganic chemical			
Ammonium sulphate (Sulphate of ammonia)	Sulphur	Feb. to June	Fairly quick acting; may be used as compost activators
Ammonium nitrate* (Nitrate of ammonia)		March to June	
Nitro-chalk Nitrate of Soda (Sodium Nitrate)	Calcium Sodium	Feb. to June March to June	As above; useful on acid soils Good on light soils, not clay. Caustic to leaves. Very quick acting
Synthetic chemical			
Urea*		March to Aug.	Very quick acting when sprayed on to foliage. Care needed in use
Organic			
Dried blood	Trace elements	March to July	Quick acting
Hoof and horn meal	Trace elements	Jan. to April	Steady release of nutrient
Bone meal	Phosphorus, Calcium	Feb. to May	Fairly quick acting
Fish meal	Phosphorus, Calcium	Feb. to May	Fairly quick acting

PHOSPHORUS is needed in all plant growth processes, root development and ripening of flowers and seeds

Inorganic			
Basic slag	Calcium	Oct. to Jan.	Slow acting; buy in finely ground form; good liming agent for acid soils
Ground rock* phosphate	Calcium	Sept. to Feb.	Lasts 3–5 years in soil. Good for acid soils
Superphosphate	Calcium, Sulphur	Feb. to June	Quick acting but long lasting; work in to

Triple superphosphate*	Calcium	Feb. to June	Oct. to March	Concentrated source of phosphorus
Organic Bone meal	Nitrogen, Calcium		Oct. to March	Excellent for planting new stock, except for lime-intolerant species. Use only sterilised or steamed bone meal

POTASSIUM is needed for sturdy growth, disease-resistance, strong growing points and flower colour. All the sources listed except powdered seaweed are quick-acting and long lasting

Inorganic			
Muriate of potash* (Potassium chloride)	Sodium	Any time	Use granulated form; do not use on clay soils
Sulphate of potash* (Potassium sulphate)	Sulphur	Any time	Best form for general use; not readily leached
Chilean potash nitrate	Sodium	Feb. to June	For liquid feeding crops, flowers and fruits; suits light soils
Wood ashes	Calcium	Any time	High lime content; keep dry before use
Inorganic chemical			
Nitrate of potash (Potassium nitrate, saltpetre)	Nitrogen	March to Aug.	Diluted liquid feed for pot and greenhouse crops and plants
Organic Powdered seaweed	Nitrogen/Phosphorus trace elements	Any time	Good soil conditioner

Other useful fertilisers are:

Epsom salts, which contain Magnesium and Sulphur and should be used when necessary in the growing season to prevent progressive dying of older leaves. Particularly good for tomatoes and potatoes.

Ferrous (Iron) sulphate, a source of iron and sulphur which can be used at any time of year to acidify chalk and lime soils. Also controls moss.

* indicates very high proportion of chief nutrient element

Organic fertilisers are held to be more gentle and benign in effect, integrating more beneficially with the soil, and releasing their nutrient elements with a steady persistence over a longer period. The exception is dried blood which is quicker-acting. Organic fertilisers tend to be expensive. Inorganic chemical fertilisers are often of granular structure, which eases distribution and slows their nutrient release over a longer period in the soil.

Fertilisers supplying one main nutrient are known as straight. Those that supply more than one nutrient are compound. The table on pp. 50–1 surveys available fertilisers and describes their effects.

☐ Apply balanced compound fertilisers as base fertilisers to seed-beds, borders or plots made ready for bedding or planting out. It is possible to mix these at home from combinations of straight fertilisers, but they must be thoroughly blended. A typical good general fertiliser, suitable for all crops and plants is one of 6 parts by weight superphosphate, 5 parts ammonium sulphate, 2 parts sulphate of potash, 1 part sulphate of magnesium, and 1 part fine bone meal, which can be used at 55–110g/m² (2–4oz per sq. yd). It has an analysis ratio of 7:9:7, meaning 7% Nitrogen, 9% Phosphorus (as phosphoric acid) and 7% Potassium (as potassium oxide).

Use proprietary compound fertilisers according to the maker's instructions, erring, if anything, on the side of deficiency to avoid waste and overdosage. It is often advantageous to supplement a base application with a smaller dose later, ensuring that more food gets through to the plant.

Modern fertilisers are expertly blended mixtures of ingredients balanced and tailored to suit specific garden crops and needs. Their granular form makes distribution easier and releases their nutrients in the soil slowly and evenly.

THE FLOWER GARDEN

Lift the roots and crowns of hardy, perennial herbaceous plants for division and replanting on bright days after recent rain. Some plants break up easily in the hands, but thick roots, rhizomes and crowns need to be severed cleanly with a sharp

Use 2 forks back-to-back to divide clumps of herbaceous plants

spade or large knife. See that each division has several buds, shoots and roots.

Discard old, worn-out centre parts. Replant as soon as possible. If delayed, cover the roots with damp sacking to prevent them drying out. Among plants eligible are achillea (*A. filipendulina*), anemone (summer- and autumn-flowering species), aster, Christmas rose (*Helleborus niger*), delphinium *Dicentra spectabilis*, fleabane (*Erigeron speciosus*), *Filipendula* species, gaillardia (*G. aristata*), golden rod (*Solidago × arendsii* varieties), hosta, lobelia (*L. syphilitica*), oenothera, phlox (*P. maculata, P. paniculata*), polygonum (*P. affine*), potentilla (*P. aurea*), speedwell (*Veronica spicata*), and periwinkle (*Vinca major, V. minor*).

☐ Stop pernicious perennial weeds running amok by painting early shoots with a systemic weedkiller in gel form to avoid it getting on garden plants. The weeds will be much more difficult to treat later when garden plants are established.

☐ Lift established montbretia (*Crocosmia*) early in the month; replant the largest corms for flowering this year, and discard the remainder. Plant new corms 7.5cm (3in.) deep in a sunny position in well-drained soil, and try a few of the related and hardier *Crocosmia masonorum* in similar conditions, 10cm (4in.) deep.

Gladiolus Primulinus hybrids left in the soil over winter should be lifted carefully with a fork. Replant the large new corms on good open ground. The tiny corms or spawn can be planted in rows 4cm (1½in.) deep in a nursery bed, where they can grow on to flowering size.

☐ Plant bulbs of the South African spire lily (or summer hyacinth), *Galtonia candicans*, as soon as they are available, 15cm (6in.) deep and the same distance apart in loamy, well-drained soil for summer flowering.

Begin planting bulbs of hardy lilies now available in well-prepared freely-drained soil. Most Asiatic lilies, their varieties and hybrids, are basal and stem-rooting, so plant them deep at 20–25cm (8–10in.), and enrich the topsoil liberally with well-rotted leaf-mould or organic materials and bone meal.

☐ Set out young sturdy plants of shasta daisies (*Chrysanthemum maximum* and hybrids), biennial and perennial campanulas, hollyhock, pyrethrum, and sweet williams from the last week of the month.

Plant out autumn-sown sweet pea seedlings, raised in a cold greenhouse or frame, with a little disturbance to the roots as possible.

Take young basal cuttings, 7.5–10cm (3–4in.) long, from the crowns of delphiniums and lupins as they start into growth. Break them off gently at their base and insert in sandy loam or a potting compost in a cold frame or under cloches in a warm border.

☐ Make a start with sowings of hardy annuals when the soil dries out and warms up late in the month. Choose a sunny position, and dress the soil with a general fertiliser, fine bone meal or superphosphate, raked in. Sow thinly, and cover the seeds lightly with sand or sifted soil. Hardy kinds include alyssum, candytuft, *Chrysanthemum carinatum* and its varieties, *Clarkia elegans*, *Convolvulus tricolor*, *Coreopsis tinctoria*, cornflower, *Euphorbia marginata*, godetia, *Gypsophila elegans*, helichrysum, larkspur (*Delphinium consolida*), love-in-a-mist (*Nigella damascena*), mallow (*Lavatera trimestris*), marigold (*Calendula officinalis*), mignonette (*Reseda odorata*), *Nemophila menziesii*, night-scented stock (*Matthiola bicornis*), and toadflax (*Linaria* species).

☐ Mark non-flowering leafy clumps of daffodils and narcissi for lifting, dividing and replanting when foliage yellows and dies. Clumps with diminishing and sparse leaves should be lifted and inspected for bulb rot caused by narcissus flies and their larvae.

THE VEGETABLE GARDEN

Dress seed-beds with a balanced base fertiliser, appropriate to the crop to be grown, and rake it in, as soon as frosts depart and soil can be worked to an even crumbly finish.

☐ Continue sowings of broad beans, longpod or Windsor varieties, white or green seeded, for a succession of crops.

Sow second early peas: 'Onward' and 'Hurst Green Shaft',

both growing to 60–75cm (2–2ft 6in.); or 'Achievement' and 'Miracle', reaching 1.2–1.5cm (4–5ft). Sow 'Recette' and 'Sweetness', 60–90cm (2–3ft), for petit-pois type peas suitable for freezing.

☐ When soil temperatures can be maintained at 13°C (55°F), make sowings in nursery beds or cold frames of brassicas, leeks, Brussels sprouts, lettuces and celeriac. Recommended varieties include: Brussels sprouts 'Peer Gynt', for autumn cropping; 'Roodnerf Rido', 'Rampart' for Christmas and 'Bedford Marsters Special' for late crops; cabbage 'Golden Acre', 'Greyhound', 'Hispi', and 'Winnigstadt' for summer/autumn cutting; Savoy cabbage 'Celtic' and 'January King' for the winter. Leeks, such as 'Lyon', 'Prizetaker' and 'Musselburgh', give crops from early winter into spring. Reliable varieties of lettuce of the smooth butterhead variety include 'Fortune' and 'All the Year Round', for crinkle-leafed, crisp-hearted lettuces choose from 'Avoncrisp', 'Webb's Wonderful' and 'Windermere', and for long-leafed cos, 'Lobjoits Green', 'Little Gem' and 'Winter Density' (a type between cos and cabbage).

☐ Grow radish as a catch crop between peas, beans and brassicas. Sow at two- to three-week intervals in shallow drills in moist humus-rich soil, giving a liquid feed for quick growth. Good varieties are 'Cherry Belle', globe-shaped; 'Saxa', round, and 'Long White Icicle', white, tapering.

☐ Sow onions in well-prepared rich soil as soon as conditions permit. 'Ailsa Craig', 'Bedfordshire Champion', 'James Long-Keeping' are globular; 'A1 White Spanish', round and flat; 'Rijnsburger Balstora' keeps well. Sow 'White Lisbon' for salad onions. Welsh onion is an interesting, useful perennial that grows in clusters like shallots.

☐ Give carrots a deep, porous soil, enriched with humus for a previous crop, and sow thinly in drills 23–30cm (9–12in.) apart; choose from 'Early Nantes', 'Chantenay Red-cored', 'Early Champion Scarlet Horn', of the stump-rooted varieties; 'Autumn King', 'James's Scarlet Intermediate', and 'St Valery' for main crops.

☐ Make main sowings of round spinach ('Hurst's 101', 'Monarch Long Standing', 'Supergreen') on humus-rich, moisture-retentive soil, in drills 30cm (12in.) apart, placing seed capsules containing up to three seeds each 15cm (6in.) apart and thinning to one seedling later.

☐ Salsify ('Mammoth', 'Sandwich Island') is a sweet piquant root vegetable, hardy enough to leave in the ground until needed in late winter–early spring. Sow this month and next thinly in drills 38cm (15in.) apart, thinning to 15cm (6in.) apart at seedling stage; they will grow in any reasonably good soil.

☐ Sow turnips ('Snowball', 'Golden Ball', 'Manchester Market', 'Milan White') towards the end of the month in drills 30cm (12in.) apart and thin the seedlings to 15cm (6in.) apart.

☐ Sow parsley ('Moss Curled', 'Green Velvet', 'Paramount') thinly in rows 25–30cm (10–12in.) apart, in good, moisture-retentive, light loam soil, and partial shade. Give them up to six weeks to germinate, and thin the seedlings to 15cm (6in.) apart.

☐ Plant sprouted seed tubers of early potatoes ('Duke of York', 'Maris Bard', 'Pentland Javelin', 'Arran Pilot', 'Foremost') in late March, about 30–38cm (12–15in.) apart in drills 15cm (6in.) deep, and rows 45cm (18in.) apart. The plot should have organic manure well worked in, and be dressed with a complete general fertiliser. Draw the soil over flat and firm it down. Cover with a sheet of black polythene, tucked into the soil along the edges, with a cross-cut slit for each tuber's shoots to grow through. This prevents frost damage, encourages early maturity and eliminates earthing-up.

☐ Lift and split clumps of chives. Replant the finest bulbs, 7.5cm (3in.) apart, in the kitchen garden. Plant others in pots in moist compost, and place on the kitchen windowsill.

☐ Remove loose litter and weeds from established asparagus beds. Dress with a general fertiliser at 60g/m² (2oz per sq. yd).

THE FRUIT GARDEN

Plant any new fruit trees as soon as possible. Soak roots overnight in a muddy slurry of water and soil. Leave unpruned and uncropped for their first year so that the roots can become established.

Withhold inorganic fertilisers from fruit trees planted in the dormant season, but mulch with organic materials after rain.

☐ Cut down newly planted raspberry canes to 10cm (4in.) stubs to get strong fruiting canes for next year.

Prune newly planted red currant and gooseberry bushes hard, by cutting back the branches by about half their length. Black currants should be cut back to 5cm (2in.) of the ground immediately after planting.

☐ Plant out maiden strawberries (last year's well-rooted runners) this month and next. Remove flower buds to build up robust fruiting crowns for the next three to four years.

☐ Apply base fertilisers as soon as possible, with the emphasis on potassium for dessert apples and gooseberries; and on nitrogen for cooking apples, pears and black currants. Boost raspberries and strawberries with organic nitrogen (dried blood, hoof and horn meal) and potassium (powdered seaweed) now, with bone meal in the autumn. Mulch all fruits over their root reach with organic material such as compost, peat, spent hops, dried sewage, spent mushroom compost, chopped straw or weathered sawdust. Apply after rain, late in the month.

☐ Examine young shoots on black currants for abnormally swollen buds, characteristic symptoms of infestation by 'big bud' mites. If present, remove and burn the buds. Spray the bushes with a 3 per cent solution of lime sulphur when the flower buds show purple at the 'grape bud' stage, and the leaves are the size of a 5p coin, in late March or early April, to stop the mites spreading.

☐ Spray pears against scab with a captan or systemic fungicide when buds begin to swell.

Black currant shoot infected by big bud on left, healthy shoot on right

THE ORNAMENTAL GARDEN

Hedges
Finish planting deciduous hedges this month. Soak the roots of plants overnight if dry. After planting, firm soil over the roots

well, and water liberally. Prune top-growth back by a half to two-thirds to encourage branching low down.

☐ Start planting evergreen and coniferous hedges and screens towards the end of the month in the south and mild districts, providing temperatures have started to rise and there is no danger of frost. Otherwise defer to April–May.

If a hedge is needed to form a barrier, consider one of the spiny barberries. *Berberis darwinii* (with rich yellow flowers), *B.* × *stenophylla* (with golden yellow flowers) and *B. julianae* (yellow flowers) are evergreen and 2m (6–7ft) or more; *B. candidula*, *B. gagnepainii*, *B. hookeri*, *B.* × *stenophylla* 'Corallina', and *B. wilsoniae* make low mounded hedges, good for garden divisions and open-plan gardens; *B. thunbergii* and *B. t.* 'Atropurpurea' make good deciduous thickets.

Lawns

Finish preparing the soil for sowing a new lawn as soon as conditions permit. Tread loose soil firm by walking in short steps on your heels over the surface. Apply a balanced lawn fertiliser at half the normal dosage. Rake level. Do not be tempted to sow too soon, but wait until April.

☐ Apply a compound lawn fertiliser to established turf this month. Use a proprietary brand or the St Ives Turf Research Station's blend: 15 parts by weight ammonium sulphate, 15 parts dried blood, 40 parts fine bone meal, 25 parts superphosphate, 5 parts sulphate of potash.

Mow to keep pace with growth, cutting rather high – at about 2cm ($\frac{3}{4}$in.).

Use the roller to true the surface, not to iron out levels. Roll lightly, when the surface is dry, after frosts.

☐ Examine browning patches of loose, dying grasses for leather-jackets – greyish-brown to black, cylindrical, tough-skinned larvae of the crane fly (daddy-long-legs) – just below the surface. Treat the area with an insecticidal dust based on derris, sevin or HCH (lindane), mixed with 2 to 3 times as much sand for even distribution.

If you don't find leather-jackets, browning spots and blotches where grasses are dying back could be due to a fungus or mould infection such as fusarium patch. Hollow-tine fork the area, and treat with a lawn fungicide.

The Rock Garden

Set out new alpine specimens now and during April using plants from pots, making sure the roots are not cramped nor drainage impaired.

☐ Raise dwarf hardy annuals for summer colour by sowing seeds in trays or seed-pans in a cold frame or greenhouse, such as *Alyssum maritimum* 'Little Dorrit', 'Rosie O'Day' and 'Snow Carpet'; *Antirrhinum* 'Little Gem', *Iberis umbellata* 'Dwarf Fairy Mixed'; *Linanthus grandiflorus* hybrids, *Linaria maroccana* 'Fairy Bouquet'; *Mesembryanthemum criniflorum*, and the 'Petite' strain of *Tagetes patula*.

Sow seeds of dwarf alpine perennials in the same way. Popular plants are *Achillea tomentosa*, *Alyssum montanum*, *Arabis alpina*, *Arenaria montana*, *Aubrieta deltoidea*, *Calandrinia umbellata*, *Campanula arvatica*, varieties of *Iberis sempervirens*, *Cerastium tomentosum*, *Dianthus alpinus* and *D. deltoides* (maiden pinks), *Leontopodium alpinum* (edelweiss), *Primula denticulata*, varieties of *Saxifraga moschata* (mossy saxifrage) and *Silene schafta*.

☐ Sprinkle a thin ring of a powdered mixture of equal parts by weight copper sulphate and ground limestone around plants to protect them from slugs and snails on damp nights, or place traps of half-coconut shells, citrus fruit rinds or halves of small flower pots, with a little slug bait or beer inside, near rock bases and crevices.

Roses

Prune established roses by the end of the month. Begin by cutting out all dead, diseased and frost-browned or split growth entirely. Cut weak and thin shoots to a robust outward-facing bud near their base. Next, prune last year's shoot growth, hard or light according to type of rose and subsequent growth required. Cut back hard, by up to two-thirds, if you want large blooms on strong stems for showing purposes; prune more moderately for more roses for garden display. The cluster-flowered roses (floribunda, polyantha) are pruned more gently than the large-flowered (HT) kinds. Cut cleanly just above outward-facing buds, with cuts slanting slightly down from the buds, leaving no stub of wood.

Cut back older shoots only if there are strong new buds or lateral shoots to which cuts can be made. On strongly growing bushes, one or more of the older branches can be removed entirely to encourage new shoots from the base. The key factor is a healthy working graft union just below soil level.

☐ Prune shrub roses and hedge roses lightly, reducing last year's shoots by up to a quarter of their length, except when new growth is needed from lower down the plants; then cut to just above a well-placed bud or young lateral shoot.

☐ Prune standard roses lightly after their first year, simply cutting last year's shoots back by a third to a half, to well-placed new buds, never to their base. Weeping standards should have been pruned in autumn with the ramblers (see November notes). Burn all the prunings to reduce the risk of spreading disease.

The correct pruning cut (extreme right) is clean, close to the bud and slopes slightly away from it. The others are jagged, too close to the bud, and too steeply angled

☐ Apply a dressing of a balanced rose fertiliser and organic mulch.

☐ Choose low-growing, non-competitive carpeting plants to cover your rose bed for added attraction. Suitable species are varieties of *Alyssum saxatile* (yellow,) *Arabis albida* (white), *Cardamine trifolia* (white), *Lysimachia nummularia* (yellow), *Primula auricula* (many colours), *Saxifraga geum* (white), *S. hypnoides* (creamy-white) and *S. umbrosa* (pink) and varieties of *Viola cornuta* (lavender). All are hardy evergreen perennials and relieve winter drabness.

Shrubs
Take extra care with late planting of deciduous shrubs this month; the sap is rising and buds soon start bursting as the days get warmer. Place the roots in water overnight; plant firmly and soak the rooting area after planting. Syringe or hose top growth if a dry spell of weather comes soon after planting.

☐ Give newly planted specimens of *Camellia sasanqua*, *Caryopteris × clandonensis*, *Ceratostigma* species, *Cestrum* species, *Choisya ternata*, *Ceanothus* species, *Desfontainea spinosa*, *Hibiscus syriacus*, varieties of *Hydrangea macrophylla*, *H. villosa*, *Indigofera gerardiana*, *Mahonia* × 'Charity', *Pittosporum* species and *Romneya* species, a protective covering of bracken, straw, tents of sacking, polythene, or plastic sheeting, or boxes, in frosty weather. When they get established they are generally hardy so this precaution may only be necessary for the first few winters.

☐ Cut back winter-flowering forms of *Erica herbacea* syn *E. carnea* during late March to May, as the flowers fade; they can be trimmed with shears to maintain neat hummocky plants, but do not cut into older brown stems, which regenerate poorly. Mark old straggly plants for replacement.

Prune other winter-flowering shrubs only if necessary to promote new shoots or to shape plants. *Chimonanthus praecox* needs no pruning in the open, but against a wall lateral shoots can be cut back to within two buds of their base after flowering. Prune witch hazels (*Hamamelis* species) and bush honeysuckles (*Lonicera standishii*, *L. fragrantissima*, *L.* × *purpusii* to shape only when young, or to thin out weak straggly shoots.

Shorten shoots of *Artemisia abrotanum*, and *A. arborescens* if compact bushes are wanted, cutting last year's growth back almost to the base. *Santolina* species (cotton lavender) can be sheared or cut hard back now, to maintain compact bushy growth of its silvery-grey foliage.

Prune hard *Buddleia davidii* and its varieties, cutting last year's flowered shoots almost to the base, to promote large flowers on arching stems this year. *B. globosa*, however, only needs the longer shoots slightly shortened.

☐ Thin varieties of *Potentilla fruticosa* by cutting the older bare shoots back to base every third year.

☐ Begin planting evergreen shrubs, trees and conifers in the last week of the month in southern and warm localities, but leave until April or May in the north.

Walls

Check over the security of supports, vine-eyes and wires, trellis, netting and lead-headed nails, if used.

Prune clematis where necessary to restrict their spread. The simple rule is to prune summer- and autumn-flowering kinds, such as *Clematis jackmanii*, *C. tangutica*, *C. orientalis* and large-

flowered hybrids, before the month is out, cutting back last
year's flowered shoots to within a few buds of their base. Leave
spring- and early-summer-flowering kinds alone.

Cut the flowered secondary shoots of the passion-flower
(*Passiflora caerulea*) back to just above a good bud near their
base, and shorten over-long leading shoots by up to a third.

Work over winter-flattened and crusted soil in wall borders
lightly with a fork and dress with a little complete fertiliser and
organic mulch.

The Water Garden
Do not feed fish until the water temperature is rising and the
fish themselves are active; then feed sparingly at first, no more
than the fish can take at a time, preferably early in the morning.
When warm weather sets in, a second feed later in the day is
welcome.

☐ Clean up established pools by thinning and pruning plants as
they show signs of budding new growth. Remove old stems,
decaying leaves and spent growth, but leave bottom silt and
mud largely undisturbed where there are fish. A light 'coating'
of limestone grit can be dropped through the water to clean it
and tidy the bottom.

☐ Prevent water greening with algae growth by floating flat
pieces of wood or cork in open spaces until plants make leaf
growth. The natural remedy is a balance of surface-leafing,
marginal and underwater plants.

☐ Repair leaking concrete pools by carefully examining the
walls above the sunken level of the water for cracks and
crumbling crevices. Chisel and scrape away loose material, and
then fill in with a waterproofing bituminous paste. Paint the
walls with a solution of the same material, letting it dry
completely before refilling the pool. If a pool has drained
through a leak in the base, it will need to be emptied of plants
and relined (see April notes).

☐ Complete the construction of a new pool, ready for April–
May planting. Neutralise the alkalinity from free lime in the
walls of cement-lined or repaired pools by painting with a
bituminous or chlorinated rubber paint, or sealing with a
solution of sodium silicate (water-glass) or proprietary product.

THE GARDEN UNDER GLASS

Continue sowings under cloches (see February notes). Dwarf
French beans are worth sowing now. Good varieties include
'Canadian Wonder', 'Loch Ness' and 'Tendergreen'. Catch-crop
with radishes.

Continue sowings in cold frames, adding dwarf French
beans. Seedlings of ten-week stocks, china asters and petunias
can also be raised from sowings made late in the month.

Greenhouse Gardening

Be guided by temperatures in greenhouse gardening this month.
For germinating seeds, rooting cuttings and getting plants into
active growth a temperature in the rooting medium or soil
should be 13–18°C (55–65°F), while the air temperature can fall
at night to 10–13°C (50–55°F) with reasonable safety. A
thermometer giving maximum/minimum readings is most
useful. Place it in the mid-area of the greenhouse, between, not
near or under, ventilators and away from the door and glass, so
as to obtain the most helpful readings.

☐ Make main sowings of hardy and half-hardy annuals for
planting out in May or early June (see February notes for
techniques and temperatures). If no source of bottom heat is
available, place seed containers near the glass on sunny days to
warm up before sowing, or defer sowing until the end of the
month or April.

☐ Regulate ventilation in step with daily temperature, opening
an hour or two before noon as temperatures rise to mid-
afternoon, closing before cool of evening. Regulate the amount
of opening according to daily temperatures, wind force and
direction. Given the choice, open ventilators on the lee side only
in strong winds.

To provide an automatic ventilation system, install louvred
ventilators near ground level and an electric extractor fan linked
with thermostatic control of temperatures.

Fit hinged ventilation lights with automatic openers,
responsive to change in temperature.

Watering. Regulate watering depending upon the growth of the
plants and atmospheric conditions. Briefly, the more actively
plants are growing, the more water they take up and transpire.
As growth activity is relative to light intensity and temperature,

it follows that the warmer and brighter the day, the more water plants need. On cloudy or rainy days with cooler temperatures, give less water, and much less still in humid weather. Overwatering is more harmful than under, especially for young plants, since it reduces the soil air available.

☐ An automatic water system saves time and labour but requires careful supervision. Of the many methods available, the most adaptable to small greenhouses are trickle and drip lines, whereby water is fed from a tank through pipes to which small diameter plastic tubes can be attached and led to individual plants to feed them with water gradually but constantly. An alternative is to lay perforated tubes between plants to supply water in a fine spray or jet. Use a moisture meter to test soils, and regulate the supply accordingly.

☐ Always keep the water supply clean. Mains water is usually suitable, feeding a tank inside the greenhouse. Rainwater should be gathered in a non-transparent container to stop it becoming green with algae and turning the soil green. It is useful to have a tank inside the greenhouse, so that water can warm to the inside temperature before use.

The Cool Greenhouse
With an average house temperature at night of 7–10°C (45–50°F), and given bottom heat of 13–18°C (55–65°F) sowings of half-hardy and hardy annuals will produce young plants for bedding out from mid-May onwards.

☐ Sow primula seeds of the polyanthus, primrose, and candelabra varieties for planting out in late May where they are to flower next year.
　　Sow seeds of pansies (*Viola* hybrids) to provide summer and autumn bloom.
　　Sow seeds of hardy perennials in late March–April, in half-trays, or singly in small peat-wood fibre pots or blocks.
　　To have flowering pot plants for the greenhouse or indoor decoration make sowings of *Browallia speciosa* and its varieties, gloxinia (*Sinningia speciosa*), *Kalanchoë blossfeldiana*, *Primula kewensis*, *P. malacoides*, *P. obconica*, *P. sinensis* and *P. stellata*, *Schizanthus* hybrids (butterfly flower), *Streptocarpus × hybridus* and *Torenia fournieri*.

☐ Pot tubers of the climbing glory lilies (*Gloriosa superba*, *G. rothschildiana*) in 20-cm (8-in.) pots about 5cm (2in.) deep. Water sparingly at first, then freely, and provide ample light and warmth.

☐ Make a start with refurbishing house plants now starting to make new growth. With mature evergreen foliage plants – aralia, cissus, fatsia, ficus, ivy and philodendrons – in good heart, simply check for good drainage, and renew the top inch or two of soil with fresh compost. Pot on to a larger size pot only if the roots are crowded, or repot in the same size pots, with fresh compost. Remove spent flowers from indoor azaleas and keep the plants growing in cool conditions, with regular waterings, until they can be placed in shady shelter out of doors for the summer.

☐ Propagate zonal pelargoniums for flowering next winter by taking cuttings this month. Select short sturdy shoots, 5–7cm (2–2½in.) long. Cut below a node or leaf and allow the cuttings to dry overnight. Insert them in a porous compost, withholding water until they are actively growing.

☐ Sow seeds of outdoor cucumber, and marrow or courgette seeds in peat-wood fibre pots or blocks singly, when temperatures are rising above 18°C (65°F) daily, for planting out in late May or early June.

☐ Mist-spray seedling plants now growing freely from earlier sowings, on warm days, preferably before noon.

☐ Strawberries brought in for forcing should be fed with a dilute balanced liquid manure twice or three times a week now; support fruit trusses with small sticks or twigs.

☐ Keep a keen watch for aphids (greenfly), especially underneath leaves, and be ready to dust or spray immediately with a derris or pyrethrum insecticide, or to water the plants with a systemic insecticide.

Peat treatment:

Alchemilla
Heathers - callunas & ericas.
Azaleas
Flame of the forest.
Magnolia - don't dig or plant anything close to the stem.
Mini - rhododendron (mauve).
Holly.
Daphne.

Buddleia - needs hard pruning. Cut back last year's growth to within 2" of the old wood.

Calluna heather - lightly clip, to remove dead flowers. Prune back straggly stems.

Jasmine - Cut back all side shoots which have flowered. Thin out some of the old branches.

Leycesteria - cut back all old & damaged shoots to a few inches above ground level.

Potentilla bushes - remove old & weak branches.

Spireas - Cut back the stems to a few inches above the ground. Annual pruning essential.

Cotoneaster horizontalis - remove unwanted or damaged branches if necessary.

April

Some April plants in flower and vegetables in season

The Flower Garden ~~trim off~~
Alyssum ~~dead~~
Arnebia ~~blooms~~
Aubrieta ~~with~~
Bergenia ~~scissors~~
Daffodils ~~to ensure~~
Doronicum ~~continuous~~ ~~flowering~~
  (leopard's
  bane)
Epimedium
Erythronium
  (dog's tooth
  violet)
Euphorbia
Fritillaria
Gentian
Grape hyacinth
Hyacinth
Leucojum
  (snowflake)
Lily of the
  valley
Narcissus
Omphalodes
Peltiphyllum
Periwinkle
Primula
Saxifraga
Tulip
Wallflower

The Ornamental Garden
Amelanchier
Berberis
Broom
Chaenomeles
  (flowering
  quince,
  japonica)
Choisya
  (Mexican
  orange)
*Clematis
  armandii*
Daphne
Dogwood
Flowering crab
  apple
Forsythia
Fothergilla
Kerria (Jew's
  mallow)
Magnolia
Maple
Pieris
Prunus
Rhododendrons
Ribes (flowering
  currant)
*Skimmia
  japonica*
Spirea
Viburnum

The Water Garden
Marsh marigold
Orontium
  (golden club)

Vegetables in season
Asparagus
Broccoli
Cabbage
Lettuce (early)

April is renowned for its variable weather and temperatures. As the days lengthen the sun's light and heat rays grow stronger, the plant world surges into the most active phase of its annual cycle. As a result plants are at their most vulnerable, since night temperatures, after days of clear blue skies and uplifting sun, can plummet below freezing point in damaging radiation frosts.

April often earns its reputation for showery, changeable weather, although statistically it averages out as a dry month. In many parts of Britain it is the driest month of the year, and gardeners need to check that young plants do not dry out.

Differences in latitude in temperate regions are now of less acute importance in determining when best to do things. The month is a busy one of seed-sowing, planting, and growth regulation, and in the colder localities of the north and on high ground, operations out of doors may only need to be delayed seven to ten days behind the average timings for the southern counties and warm areas given in these notes.

Frosts. In April and May early plant growth and flowers, particularly fruit blossom, are easily damaged by radiation frosts. These are apt to occur in periods of high barometric pressure when clear starlit nights follow days of warming sunshine. At nightfall, the earth and its vegetation radiate back much of the heat absorbed during the day. The air above them is warmed and rises. Heavier colder air moves in to take its place, flowing in much the same way as water would from high ground to low. In the morning, the white rime of ground frost marks its passage and effect, where it filled the hollows, and finally built up in depth at the lowest levels, reaching vulnerable plants.

To prevent radiation frost damage, it is necessary to interpose a barrier or cover between susceptible plants and the open sky. Cloches, tents of hessian, sheet polythene, netting, or even newspaper will all serve to prevent warm air from rising and keep the area around vulnerable growing points and buds above freezing level. It also helps to facilitate the flow of air from high to low ground by keeping hedge bottoms open at the base if they are sited across the slope and when possible, placing hedges, fences or walls to deflect the flow of air rather than halt it. On low ground, plant only frost-hardy subjects or grow tall shrubs and trees that will carry their shoots and flowers out of reach of ground frosts.

Damage to frost-touched growing points and tissues can be minimised by spraying the plants with tepid water in the early morning before the sun's rays fall upon them. It is morning sun (and thaw) after frost which harms the plants rather than the frost itself.

Weeds. Any plant that grows where the gardener does not want it is a weed, but in practice the term defines non-ornamental varieties that are so vigorous that, left unchecked, would smother cultivated plants. Keep down weeds among crops and plants assiduously. Give seeds a good start by thorough preparation of the seed beds. The application of a pre-emergent weedkiller destroys germinating weed seedlings then loses toxicity before slower-germinating seedlings break through. Timing is critical, so follow the maker's instructions precisely.

Master the use of the hoe for weeding. Use a sharp Dutch hoe, with a shallow push–pull action to decapitate annual weeds and top-growth. Mix weed remains with the soil. Hand weed and fork out perennial weeds or chop them out with a draw hoe.

☐ Mulch flower and shrub borders, under fruit and ornamental bushes and trees to smother weeds. Tread or beat the green top-growth flat, and cover with an inch or so of moist peat, compost, forestry bark or weathered sawdust, to within a few inches of the base of plants.

☐ Use weedkillers carefully among plants, wetting the weed foliage and stems only, by means of a sprinkler bar or hooded sprayer held directly over the weeds. A paraquat-diquat herbicide is most effective against annual weeds and the green top-growth of most other weeds; dalapon can be used for couch and other grasses and 2, 4-D, mecoprop, or ioxynil for various broad-leaved weeds. Choose a dry, calm day when rain or frost is not imminent for using weedkiller solutions. Spot–treatment is essential in situations such as lawns and rockeries where the weedkiller must not fall on surrounding plant life. Weedkiller in gel form can easily be confined to weeds and should be applied with a brush.

Spot-treating weeds

Fungicides. Apply fungicides wisely. These chemical substances designed to prevent or halt the attack of fungus diseases on plants are toxic chiefly to germinating spores and developing threads (hyphae) of fungi; more preventive and protectant than curative, they need to be applied immediately the first symptoms show. They may be applied as sprays or dusts. In either form, the intent must be to cover all surfaces including the undersides of leaves of the plant to give full protection. Systemic fungicides and insecticides, however, are absorbed into the tissues and sap stream of the plant to defeat infection from within. Remember that fungicides are to some degree toxic to forms of life – human, animal, insect and fish – other than parasites. A choice of suitable fungicides for specific diseases as they are likely to occur is given in the monthly notes.

☐ Not all diseases are fungal in nature. Virus diseases attack all kinds of garden plants, causing stunted growth, misshapen specimens, small fruits or none at all: in short, their effect can be devastating and the only remedy is to grub out and burn affected plants. Prevention by good cultivation methods and choosing healthy stock is essential. It also helps to keep insect pests down as some virus diseases are carried from plant to plant by vectors such as aphids.

Insecticides. Examine plants and crops frequently for parasites feeding on them, since they can increase rapidly under conditions of a suitable environment and intensive cultivation. Vigorous growth promoted by good culture; adequate spacing of plants; and good garden hygiene give plants some resistance to parasites, but effective control of outbreaks of infection or infestation largely depends on taking early action.

Tackle insects pests promptly, otherwise they increase rapidly with access to a good food supply. All insecticides are poisonous to some degree. The safest are those based on organic plant substances – derris (rotenone), pyrethrum (pyrethrin) and quassia – for use on food crops, in the greenhouse, and where there are children or pet animals. Insecticides are designed to kill insects on contact, and/or when ingested. They may also kill beneficial pollinating and predatory insects (such as bees and ladybirds) unless well timed and precisely applied. On a small scale it is effective to remove insects by hand. Specific treatments against insects in their season are given in the monthly notes.

PEST CONTROL

Thorough cultivation of the soil and good garden hygiene are essential in controlling pests. Do not leave plant debris lying around. Keep weeds down.

Use all chemicals strictly in accordance with the manufacturer's instructions, protecting hands and face as you work. Keep in a safe place away from children and pets and thoroughly wash out containers after use. Some chemicals should not be used on food plants close to harvest; take note of the manufacturer's instructions on this point.

Pests	Plants affected	Symptoms	Chemical Treatment
Apple sucker	Apples	Withered petals	Spray with BHC, dimethoate or fenitrothion after petal fall
Bean weevil	Beans	Semi-circular notches in leaves	Dust BHC or spray fenitrothion on young plants
Blackfly	Beans, nasturtiums, honeysuckle	Colonies infest new shoots, stunting growth and damaging buds	Spray with primicarb or pyrethrum
Cabbage root fly	All brassicas	Maggots eat roots, young plants collapse	Dust base of newly transplanted seedlings with pirimiphos-methyl
Capsid bugs	Fruit trees and bushes, herbaceous plants	Punctured leaves and fruit	Spray with BHC or malathion
Carrot fly	Carrots	Maggots eat roots	Use an insecticide seed-dressing

Pest	Plant	Symptoms	Treatment
Caterpillars	Vegetables, fruit bushes, hedges, flowers	Leaves eaten	Spray or dust with derris
Codling moth	Apples, pears	Grubs in fruit	Spray with fenitrothion in mid-June and 3 weeks later
Cutworms	Brassicas, beetroot, lettuce, flowers	Stems eaten through	Work BHC dust into soil
Earwigs	Chrysanthemums, dahlias	Holes in flowers and leaves	Spray or dust plants and soil with BHC
Flea beetles	Brassicas, wallflowers	Small holes on leaf surfaces	Dust seedlings with BHC or derris
Greenfly	Roses, flowers, fruit trees and bushes, vegetables	As blackfly	Spray with malathion, derris, nicotine or pyrethrum
Leaf hoppers	Fruit trees, roses, potatoes	Pale patches on leaves	Spray fortnightly with BHC, malathion or nicotine
Leaf miners	Flowers and shrubs	Larvae tunnel through leaf tissue leaving fine lines	Remove and burn affected leaves. Spray with BHC
Leather-jackets	Lawns	Brown patches; grey grubs below surface	Drench soil with pirimiphos-methyl

Pests	Plants affected	Symptoms	Chemical Treatment
Mealy bugs	Mostly in greenhouses	Small cream oval insects covered with wax on leaves	Spray thoroughly with formothion or malathion
Onion fly	Onion family	Wilting foliage, grubs in bulbs	Apply calomel dust to soil on or just after sowing
Pea moth	Peas	Maggots in pod	When the flowers open, spray with fenitrothion
Raspberry beetle	Raspberries, blackberries, loganberries	Grubs eat fruit	Spray thoroughly with derris when fruits turn pink
Red spider	Esp. in greenhouse; fruit trees and bushes, tomatoes, vines, flowering plants	Mottled leaves; red mites on underside	Spray thoroughly with derris, dimethoate or malathion
Root aphid	Lettuces, asters, pot plants	Leaves wilt	Water a solution of malathion into roots of affected plants
Sawfly	Apples, plums	Grubs in fruit	Spray with BHC immediately after petal fall
Scale insects	Fruit trees, vines, shrubs, foliage houseplants	Small flat insects under leaves, on stems	Spray with malathion
Slugs and snails	Garden and greenhouse	Seedlings destroyed; established plants badly damaged	Lay bait of metaldehyde or methiocarb

Thrips	Many garden plants esp. gladioli; also in greenhouse	Mottled and silvery leaves and flowers	Spray or dust with BHC, malathion, nicotine, or derris
Tortrix moth caterpillars	Apples, plums, trees, shrubs	Punctured leaves bound together with silvery threads	Remove by hand or spray with BHC, derris or trichlorphon
Vine weevil	Greenhouse plants esp. vines	Holes eaten in edge of leaves	Spray with BHC
Whitefly	Many garden and greenhouse plants	As blackfly	Spray with BHC, pyrethrum, malathion
Winter moth	Apples and other fruit trees	Caterpillars eat leaves and young fruits	Spray with trichlorphon, malathion or derris as buds open and leaves develop
Wireworm	Flowers, vegetables	Roots attacked by tunnelling larvae	Apply BHC to soil
Woodlice	Many garden and greenhouse plants	Holes eaten in leaves; roots also damaged	Dust nesting places with antkiller dust
Woolly aphid	Apples	White fluff on branches	Brush on or spray solution of malathion or BHC at first signs

DISEASE CONTROL

Aim to prevent disease by good garden hygiene, regular and thorough soil cultivation and growing only vigorous plants. Where a virus-free certification scheme is in operation, grow certified specimens only. Most chemicals are preventive in action. Once a disease has taken hold, remove affected plants or parts of plants, and burn them. Keep plants healthy and nourished. In using chemicals, observe the precautions given on p. 74 under Pest Control.

Diseases	Plants affected	Symptoms	Chemical treatment
Blackspot	Roses	Dark spots on leaves that turn pale and fall off	Spray regularly with benomyl, captan or zineb
Blight	Potatoes and tomatoes	Blotched leaves turn brown and rot; tubers covered in grey patches	Spray fortnightly with Bordeaux mixture, liquid copper, maneb or zineb
Botrytis (grey mould)	Especially strawberries and tomatoes; many other plants	Velvety mould on rotting leaves	Use a general garden fungicide at first sign
Cane spot	Raspberries, blackberries, loganberries	Round dark spots on stems turn white and crack open	Spray with 5% lime-sulphur at bud-burst, $2\frac{1}{2}$% just before blossom time
Chocolate spot	Broad beans	Brown blotches on leaves in summer or after December on overwintered plants	Spray young leaves with a copper fungicide
Club root	Brassicas, wallflowers, stocks	Wilting leaves, distorted swollen roots	Lime the soil; dust planting holes with 4% calomel

Damping off	Lettuces especially; many other plants	Seedlings rot and collapse	Water with Cheshunt compound, captan or zineb
Peach leaf curl	Peaches, nectarines, almonds inc. ornamental varieties	Red blisters on leaves that turn white, then brown before falling off	Spray with lime-sulphur or Bordeaux mixture in January
Petal blight	Especially chrysanthemums; also dahlias and anemones	Browning of the petals in wet seasons	Spray or dust with zineb just before the flower buds open
Powdery mildew	Many types	Pale powdery coating on leaves and shoots	Spray regularly with benomyl or dinocap
Rust	Many flowers and vegetables	Orange spores on leaves and stems	Spray fortnightly with zineb
Scab	Apples and pears	Brown scabs on fruit	Spray regularly with benomyl, captan or lime-sulphur
Tulip fire	Tulips	Shoots rot, bulbs covered in black spores	Dust bulbs and soil with quintozene before planting

THE FLOWER GARDEN

Make further sowings of hardy annuals in prepared places (see March notes). When soil temperatures exceed 15.5°C (60°F), seeds of half-hardy annuals may be sown out of doors.

☐ Sow hardy climbing annuals – *Convolvulus tricolor*, tall single-flowering nasturtiums, *Humulus scandens* (ornamental hop), *Tropaeolum peregrinum* (Canary creeper) at the base of trellises, tree stumps, banks and eyesores needing quick coverage.

☐ Lift, divide and replant crowded clumps of red hot pokers (*Kniphofia* species) now, enriching the soil with well-rotted organic matter and bone meal.

☐ Plant *Acidanthera bicolor murielae* bulbs now for September blooming. Place them 10cm (4in.) deep in loam soil in a warm, sheltered border. As they are semi-tropical, they succeed best in mild localities.
Plant the hardiest of the cape lilies, *Crinum powellii* and its varieties, in rich deep soil where they will enjoy open full sun, setting the bulbs 20cm (8in.) deep and the same distance apart.

☐ Plant gladioli corms in free-draining, well-forked soil, 10cm (4in.) deep, 15–20cm (6–8in.) apart, at 2–3 week intervals this month, for a succession of blooms into autumn. On heavy soils, plant 5–7.5cm (2–3in.) deep, set on a 1-cm ($\frac{1}{2}$-in.) layer of sand to aid drainage.
Plant border and Korean chrysanthemums from mid-April onwards, watering in well if the weather is dry.
Plant border carnations in good soil, well-laced with ground limestone if acid, and give a top mulch of limestone chippings.

☐ Plant out seedling pansies which have overwintered in a cold frame, with a dressing of slug bait. They like partial shade.
Plant out in deep soil sweet peas raised in pots. They will need the support of twiggy branches, stakes or wires stretched across posts.

☐ Plant autumn-sown antirrhinums, calendulas, clarkias, corn flowers, godetias, mignonettes and pentstemons from their wintering quarters in a sheltered seed-bed or cold frame, with the encouragement of a little superphosphate raked in beforehand.

☐ Stake the taller herbaceous perennials now making growth, or stretch 7.5cm–10cm (3–4in.) mesh plastic netting through which the plants can grow over the border on strong posts. This saves time and achieves a more natural look.

☐ Lift and divide hardy ferns that merit, it replanting the crowns singly in soil enriched with moist organic matter.

Cane and wire supports for tall herbaceous plants

THE VEGETABLE GARDEN

Make successional sowings of broad beans, carrots, second early peas, turnips, radish, lettuce and spinach (see March notes).

Provide supports for earlier sown peas when 5cm (2in.) high. Sow tall maincrops ('Lord Chancellor', 'Senator') for August cropping.

Sow sprouting broccoli ('Calabrese Green', 'Early Purple', and 'Early White'); late Brussels sprouts ('Cambridge No. 5', 'Bedford Winter Harvest', 'Bedford Fillbasket'), Savoy cabbage ('Best of All', 'Winter King'), kohl rabi ('White', 'Purple'), and Australian varieties of cauliflower in a cold frame or sheltered seed-bed, from mid-April onwards.

Sow 'Avon early' or 'Boltardy' beetroot for late summer cropping; thin seedlings to 10–15cm (4–6in.) apart as soon as large enough to handle.

☐ Plant up a new asparagus bed this month with crowns 12–15cm (5–6in.) below ground level. Raise from seeds 'Connover's Colossal' or 'Martha Washington' for next year's planting; germination is slow.

☐ Choose a patch of well-drained, sandy loam soil for annual herbs – bush basil, sweet basil, borage, chervil, coriander, dill, sweet marjoram, purslane, summer savory – and sow at the end of the month. Sow the biennials – angelica, caraway – where they can stay for two years. Sow the perennials – lemon balm, chives, fennel, hyssop, lavender, lovage, mint, rosemary, sage, winter savory, sorrel, and thyme – in pots for transplanting later in the year.

☐ Harden off seedlings of brassicas, leeks and onions raised in the greenhouse by placing them in a cold frame for a week or so and plant out firmly and water in. For an early crop, plant leek seedlings in a prepared trench, or drop them in holes made with a dibber, about 15cm (6in.) deep and 15cm apart.

☐ Earth up with a draw hoe early potatoes when their stems are up to 20cm (8in.) tall. Do not work in very wet or cold weather, for the soil should be easy to work. Repeat in 3–4 weeks.

Finish planting second early potatoes before the middle of the month and maincrops before the end, spacing them 45cm (18in.) apart, in rows 75–90cm (2ft 6in.–3ft) apart. Rub off all but two robust sprouts per tuber; cut large seed tubers with two sprouts on each piece just before planting.

Protect early shoots of potatoes with a cover of tented hessian, sheet polythene, or cloches when night frosts are forecast.

☐ Prepare celery trenches 30–40cm (12–15in.) deep; 38cm (15in.) wide for a single row, 45cm (18in.) for a double, with well-rotted compost firmed into the bottom with a dressing of fine bone meal, ready for June planting.

As celery plants make growth, tie up the heads and fill in the trench to blanch the stems

☐ Dress seedling peas damaged by leaf weevils with a derris insecticide. Treat brassica seedlings with holes and eaten leaves caused by flea beetles with a derris or an HCH dust.

THE FRUIT GARDEN

Prevent or reduce fungus infections such as early mildew, scab, canker and blossom wilt on apple and pear trees by spraying at the green bud stage with a systemic fungicide on a calm day when foliage and shoots can be covered easily and completely.

At the same time apply a systemic insecticide to control such pests as apple sawfly, moth caterpillars, aphids, capsid bug, apple blossom weevil, leaf weevils, suckers and scale insects.

Repeat the spraying when blossom buds show white on pears, pink on apples, in late April or early May.

Spray gooseberry bushes when the flowers are about to open with a systemic insecticide or dinocap formulation, to control American mildew.

☐ Examine strawberries for the presence of aphids or red spider mites (under cloches) in warm dry late-April weather, and treat with a malathion insecticide if necessary.

THE ORNAMENTAL GARDEN

Hedges
Plant evergreen hedges and screens this month and next, in well-worked soil, enriched with peat or rotted organic matter. Start with young plants as they establish themselves best.

Avoid box and yew where livestock are likely to eat their foliage; holly is a better choice in such circumstances. Conifers and holly make long-lived, easily maintained hedges where appropriate.

Remember conifers require comparatively clean country air to thrive, and do not do well in towns, or industrial areas. The hybrid × *Cupressocyparis leylandii* is the fastest-growing; for hedging choose a clone such as 'Leighton Green'. Many of the forms of *Chamaecyparis lawsoniana* are adaptable to hedging; *Thuja plicata* is more suited to the warmer half of Britain than the north, where *T. occidentalis* is preferable. *Cupressus macrocarpa* is best avoided, except in coastal districts, unless noted to be thriving.

☐ Cut back and prune overgrown and neglected box, holly, laurel and yew hedges this month, as soon as buds begin to burst. All regenerate well from quite severe treatment as long as the cuts are clean. Dress large cut surfaces with a fungicide or tree dressing.

☐ Overhead-spray newly planted and pruned hedges in dry weather. Give liquid feeds to the roots and apply a mulch to the surface rooting area.

Paths
Get rid of grass and weeds growing between flagstones of paths and paved areas by spraying with simazine, diquat or paraquat. To stop growth, scrape out soil and grout with a mixture of 1 part by volume quick-setting cement, 2 parts clean sand, and sufficient water to make a stiff porridge.

Sodium chlorate works best through the leaves of weeds in active growth and its use is best confined to waste ground. Choose a product with added fire depressant (calcium chloride) for safety. Apply in dry weather in solution, but not nearer than 38cm (15in.) to lawns and green plants, as it may 'creep', and persists for nearly a year in the soil.

Lawns
If you plan a new lawn sow it this month, with a seed mixture chosen to suit the soil, situation, and purpose, on a well-prepared site (see March notes). Dress the seeds with a bird repellent. Overhead-water if a dry spell intervenes. Most grass seeds should germinate in 10–21 days. Cut when about 5cm (2in.) high, reducing height by half.

☐ Wait until grasses and weeds are growing strongly in established lawns before applying a selective weedkiller on a dry calm day, when rain is unlikely for 24 hours. 2, 4-D herbicides control most broad-leaved weeds, but you need mecoprop for clovers, chickweed, pearlwort, self-heal, yarrow and field woodrush, and iotymil for parsley piert and speedwells. Other resistant weeds need hand-lifting or spot-treatment. Do not use cuttings from newly treated lawns for mulching or manuring or composting.

☐ Mow frequently, keeping pace with growth, but not too close unless for a play-games surface. Remove cuttings for compost, using an activator specially suited to the breaking down of such fine leaves to crumbly mould. Cylinder-cutting mowers give a smooth finish, but rotary-scything mowers trim coarse grasses and prostrate-growing weeds more effectively.

☐ Renovate a neglected lawn this month. Start by scarifying well to remove 'thatch', prostrate-running weeds, and coarse weeds, then fertilise, aerate, and sow with a seed mixture at half the normal rate, bulked with sand or sifted light loam, brushed and watered in.

The Rock Garden

Plant dwarf evergreen shrubs and dwarf conifers this month and next. Choice evergreens are *Berberis × stenophylla* 'Corallina', *Daphne sericea*, *D. retusa*, *Erica herbacea* syn. *E. carnea*, *Helianthemum alpestre*, *H. lunulatum*, varities of *H. nummularium*, *Polygala chamaebuxus*, veronicas such as *Hebe* 'Autumn Glory', and 'Bowles Hybrid'. Given a lime-free soil, the choice widens to include *Andromeda polifolia* 'Nana', *Cassiope* species, *Gaultheria miqueliana*, varieties of *Leiophyllum buxifolium*, *Pernettya tasmanica*, *Phyllodoce* species, many dwarf rhododendrons, varieties of the heather *Calluna vulgaris*, and bell heather, *Erica cinerea*, varieties of the Irish heath, *Daboecia cantabrica*, the Dorset heath, *Erica ciliaris*, and the cross-leaved heath, *E. tetralix*.

Water dwarf conifers in well and spray the foliage in dry weather. Check the height to which dwarf conifers may ultimately grow as true dwarfs are relatively few. The following are useful; *Abies balsamea* 'Hudsonia', *Chamaecyparis lawsoniana* 'Nana Lutea', *C. obtusa* 'Pygmaea', *Cryptomeria japonica* 'Vilmoriniana', *Juniperus communis* 'Compressa', *J. × media* 'Old Gold', *J. squamata* 'Blue Star', and *Thuja orientalis* 'Aurea Nana' – all distinctive, growing well in open situations and ordinary soil laced with peat.

Roses

Plant pot-grown miniature roses and water in. Prune to shape only. Complete any March tasks still outstanding as soon as possible.

Shrubs and Trees

Buy evergreen shrubs and trees with roots in a soil ball, not bare-rooted. Take care to make the planting hole large enough. Place in planting hole, remove wrapping unless readily decomposable; firm good soil mixed with moist peat or rotted organic matter around plants, and water in dry spells.

☐ If desired, plant, or transplant, magnolias this month, when growth is just beginning. Avoid injury to their fleshy roots.

☐ Nurse newly planted shrubs and trees in their first year after planting. Provide them with temporary windbreaks against drying winds, with syringing and watering in drought, with moist mulches over the rooting area, and keep free from grass and weeds.

☐ Prune summer- and autumn-flowering shrubs this month, cutting away weak and dead shoots, and cutting back other shoots to just above strong buds about to burst.

Cut out completely shoots or branches of variegated shrubs and trees which have reverted to green, whenever seen.

Go over large-flowered forms of *Hydrangea macrophylla* to remove last year's dead flowerheads and stalks, dead wood and spindly shoots; but leave shoots of last year's growth with good terminal buds to flower this year. Protect against late frosts.

☐ Clear weeds under established shrubs and spot-treat rosette weeds such as dandelions with systemic weedkiller if they do not yield to hand weeding. Fork lightly to loosen compacted surfaces and make it easier for rain to penetrate.

Walls

Clip ivy close to walls. It is best removed from trees by severing the stems at soil level, and treating stumps with ammonium sulphamate.

☐ Prune climbing shrubs such as Virginia creeper (species of *Parthenocissus*) and ornamental vine (*Vitis coignetiae*).

☐ Plant new evergreen climbers with their roots 30–45cm (12–18in.) wide of the base of walls or fences, which tend to become very dry.

The Water Garden

Spring-clean an existing pool when the weather turns warm. Remove the fish and place them temporarily in a container filled with fresh water in partial shade, if the bottom soil is to be disturbed. Lift overgrown water lilies and aquatic plants in need of division. Discard dead and moribund parts and leaves. Keep roots moist under wet sacking until replanted, while changing or renovating slimy, silty soil. Cut away dead top-growth of marginal and bog plants. It is helpful to top replanted stock with gravel or chippings, Refill the pool gently, letting water overflow from a bucket or pan. Allow it to settle and clear before re-introducing fish.

☐ Put soil in new pools for May–June planting (see May notes). Use heavy fibrous loam or clayey topsoil, 10–15cm (4–6in.) thick. Do not use fertilisers or strong manures, except bone meal. Add broken charcoal for small pools and tub gardens, then moisten well.

☐ Check greening algae growth in clear water by shading it with floating boards. Introduce mollusc scavengers such as ramshorn snails and freshwater mussels, about four to six per square metre of pool area. The natural preventive is balanced planting (see May notes).

THE GARDEN UNDER GLASS

Make further sowings of dwarf French beans under cloches (see February and March notes). Make new sowings of sweet corn and runner beans in open ground, covered with cloches.

Greenhouse Gardening
Increase ventilation as days lengthen and grow warm; water to keep soils and composts moist; mist-spray seedlings and young plants on sunny warm days (see March notes).

Temperature differences in cold and cool greenhouses decrease as the month advances, making practices applicable to both.

☐ Prick out into pots seedlings of annuals and other plants sown earlier, as soon as large enough to handle between first finger and thumb, holding by seed leaves or first true leaves, not the fragile roots. Firm gently, give water and shade from hot sun.

☐ Pot the tubers of *Achimenes* species and hybrids, 2.5cm (1in.) deep, 5cm (2in.) apart, in good potting compost, at 15.5–21°C (60–70°F), and give ample light and air, with tepid watering to keep the compost damp.

Pot tuberous double begonias, flat or hollow side uppermost, just covered with soil, in temperatures of 13–18°C (55–65°F), for autumn flowering in the greenhouse. Start them off in boxes, 10cm (4in.) apart, using John Innes No. 1 compost, for planting out into window boxes, tubs and vases in late May–early June. Start off *B.* × *tuberhybrida* 'Pendula' varieties for baskets.

Pot bulbs of *Ornithogalum thyrsoides* (chincherinchees), 5cm (2in.) deep, five or six to a 20-cm (8-in.) pot, for late summer bloom in the greenhouse; ordinary potting composts are suitable.

☐ Sow seeds of zinnias and *Lobelia tenuior*, with bottom heat of 15.5–20°C (60–68°F). Sow seeds of cineraria (*Senecio cruentus*) under the same conditions, for winter flowering, pricking off singly into pots as soon as the first true leaves form.

☐ Sow more seeds of the cucurbits – outdoor cucumber, marrow, melon, ornamental gourd – singly in peat-wood fibre pots or blocks, with bottom heat of 18–24°C (65–75°F).

☐ Sow seeds of outdoor varieties of tomato, 2.5cm (1in.) apart in pans or trays of standard compost, giving bottom heat of 18–21°C (65–70°F). Prick off seedlings singly into small peat-wood fibre pots or peat blocks.

☐ Harden off half-hardy and hardy annuals raised under glass towards the end of the month. Place them in cold frames and expose them gradually to lower temperatures, increasing ventilation and conditions approaching those outdoors, in order to prepare them for placing in flowering positions in the open garden in May.

☐ Pot on seedlings of *Primula malacoides*, *P. obconica*, *P. sinensis*, and *P. stellata* into 10–15cm (4–6in.) pots, to be grown on under cool conditions for greenhouse and indoor decoration.

☐ If not already done, prepare greenhouse borders for the ring culture of tomatoes or cucumbers (see January notes), by removing top 5–7.5cm (2–3in.) of soil, and replacing it with moist peat or pulverised forestry bark. Place bottomless 23-cm (9-in.) fibre, plastic or clay rings containing John Innes potting compost No. 3 or a standard equivalent, on this substratum, about 38cm (15in.) apart.

Place grow-bags – plastic pillows filled with peat or pulverised forestry bark mixed with balanced compound fertilisers – on the floor of a greenhouse to warm up a few days before planting with tomatoes, capsicums, cucumbers or melons.

Water thoroughly until evenly moist throughout. It is helpful to make small drainage holes in the base at the corners of the bags to guard against waterlogging.

☐ Plant tomatoes from mid-April in a cool greenhouse, the end of April or early May in a cold house, when temperatures are 13–18°C (55–65°F). Choose sturdy plants, with the first truss of flowers about to open, of varieties suited to greenhouse cultivation – 'Alicante', 'Harbinger', 'Moneymaker', 'Eurocross', and 'Golden Sunrise'.

☐ Plant aubergines, cucumbers and melons in rings, grow-bags or 25-cm (10-in.) pots when house temperatures reach and exceed 18°C (65°F). These plants require somewhat more humid conditions than tomatoes, with liberal watering and syringing.

☐ Prick off seedlings of sweet pepper and chillies (*Capsicum annuum* and varieties) singly into 15-cm (6-in.) pots to grow on in the greenhouse.

☐ Thin the fruitlets of indoor apricots, nectarines, and peaches when they are the size of a marble. Reduce to two per shoot and then to one about three weeks later. Syringe them well on hot sunny days to repel red spider mites; and apply a malathion insecticide if seen.

☐ Feed potted-up strawberries weekly with a dilute feed. Put in supports for fruit trusses, and thin these to the best five or six when beginning to swell.

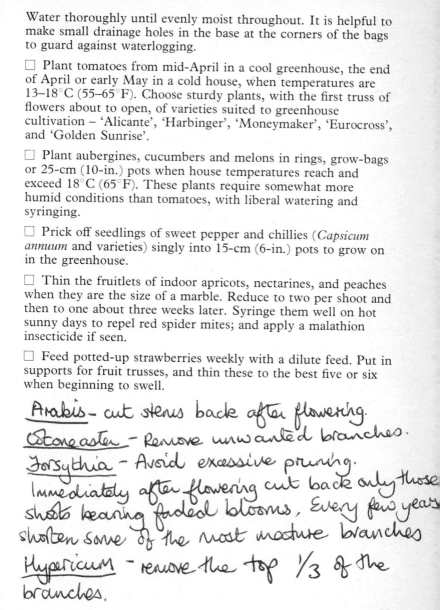

Arabis - cut stems back after flowering.

Cotoneaster - Remove unwanted branches.

Forsythia - Avoid excessive pruning. Immediately after flowering cut back only those shoots bearing faded blooms. Every few years shorten some of the most mature branches

Hypericum - remove the top ⅓ of the branches.

PTO

Lavender - (remove stalks when flowers fade?)
Trim back plants. Do not cut into old wood.
Flowering Currant - after flowering, prune back
shoots which have flowered. Cut out old,
unproductive wood.

May

Some May plants in flower and vegetables in season

The Flower Garden

Aethionema
Allium
Alyssum
Anemone
Aquilegia
  (columbine)
Arnebia
Aubrieta
Bergenia
Brunnera
Bugle
Camassia
Catmint
Dodecatheon
  (shooting star)
Doronicum
Epimedium
Erinus
Euphorbia
Fritillaria
Forget-me-not
Gentian
Geum
Gypsophila
Iris
Jacob's Ladder
  (Polemonium)
Pansy
Paeony
Peltiphyllum
  peltatum
Penstemon
Phlox
Poppy
Primula
Ranunculus
  (buttercup)
Rock rose
Saxifraga
Star of
  Bethlehem
Tiarella
Trollius
Tulip
Veronica
Vinca
Wallflower

The Ornamental Garden

Amelanchier
Azalea
Broom
Ceonothus
Choisya
Cistus
Clematis
Cotoneaster
Cytisus
Daphne
Eleagnus
Flowering crab
  apple
Hawthorn
Honeysuckle
Horse chestnut
Kerria
Kolkwitzia
Laburnum
Lilac (*syringa*)
Magnolia
Maple
Osmaria
Paeonia
Pieris
Potentilla
Prunus
Pyracantha
Rhodendron
Rosa Banksia
Sorbus
Viburnum
Wistaria

The Water Garden
Calla (bog
  arum)
Marsh marigold
Water violet
  (Holtonia)
Orontium
  (golden club)

Vegetables in season

Asparagus
Beans, broad
Cabbage, spring
Lettuce
Onion (salad)
Rhubarb
Spinach

In May, as in April, longer sunny days boost plants into increasingly active growth and warm the garden and the soil. There is always the danger at night, however, of the frosts of spring to which the British climate is liable, and which can devastate tender leaves and flowers. When the barometric pressures are high, and the winds moving from the north or east, the onset of a clear starry night is likely to bring frost, and the stronger the flow of cold air from higher to lower ground, the more damaging the frost is likely to be.

Nevertheless, daily temperatures should be mounting above 15.5°C (60°F), so there need not be much difference in the timing of gardening operations between the south and the north, as long as particular local conditions are taken into consideration. Gardens in valleys and on low-lying ground are more vulnerable to spring frosts than those on slopes. Even within a single garden, the lower parts or pockets of hollows are the worst affected. A canopy of tree branches or taller shrubs means warmer night conditions underneath. As a general guide spring planting may be carried out safely earlier in the west than in the east.

THE FLOWER GARDEN

Make additional outdoor sowings of hardy annuals where needed as soon as possible. Use a seed-dressing to improve germination.

Thin seedlings sown in April as soon as they are large enough to handle.

Move hardy and half-hardy annual seedlings sown in the greenhouse to cold frames to harden off. Close the frames at night, but increase ventilation by day in step with the temperature, watering early in the day. Transplant to flowering positions in 2–3 weeks' time.

Plant out hardened-off half-hardy annuals after rain, if possible, or water in, from mid-May, but have cloches or some form of cover available if night frosts are expected. Delay planting out until late May or early June in cold, exposed or northern gardens.

☐ Snip off faded flower heads from early-flowering bulbs and daffodils unless the seeds are needed. Leave the seed capsules on crocus and snowdrops which you want to increase naturally.

Give the plants a liquid feed of a fertiliser high in nitrogen to boost foliage and the build-up of the bulbs for next year. Wait until the foliage yellows before removing it.

☐ If spent early-flowering tulips must be lifted because their bed is needed, take them up carefully with roots and soil intact. Place in a prepared trench on spare ground, cover with soil and leave until the leaves wither, before sorting for storage.

☐ Replant indoor bulbs that have finished flowering outside in a sheltered corner. Keep them intact and let them finish growing before sorting for size and storing for outdoor planting in the autumn. They will need two to three years of growing to make top-size flowering bulbs again. Small offset bulbs and corms need to be grown on separately in fairly rich soil.

☐ Lift and split early spring-flowering plants of the *Primula* family such as polyanthus, primroses, cultivated cowslips and oxlips after flowering into rosettes of leaves with root rhizome and roots attached, and replant firmly in humus-rich soil in light shade. Water in with a weak solution of fertiliser.

☐ Plant bought-in or wintered dormant dahlia tubers in the latter half of the month, where they are to flower, but be prepared to protect them from radiation frosts especially in the north.

☐ Make final plantings of gladioli corms, and treat the soil surface with a pre-emergent weedkiller.

☐ Sow seeds of biennials for next year on a reserve seed-bed, such as Canterbury bells, honesty, wallflowers, and sweet william, to have sturdy plants for transplanting in the autumn to flower next year. Find room also to grow a few perennials from seeds such as *Alyssum saxatile*, aubrieta, delphinium, gaillardia and lupins.

☐ Renovate window-boxes for summer. Paint wooden ones inside with bitumen or a plant-safe preservative, not creosote. Cover drainage holes with plastic mesh, line boxes with an inch or so of broken crocks, brick, or gravel, then a layer of leaves, before filling with a balanced compost (John Innes No. 2 or a soil-less mixture); soak and allow to drain before planting up with a choice of annuals, dwarf pelargoniums, dahlias or begonias. A box for the kitchen windowsill could be planted with herbs.

☐ Make up hanging baskets this month. Line the old-fashioned wire ones with live moss, then fine-mesh plastic netting or perforated sheet polythene, and fill with compost. Or use modern plastic baskets which need only filling with a soil compost. Plant up as you fill, with young plants out of pots or in peat-wood fibre pots or peat blocks – such as *Asparagus plumosus*, *Begonia* Pendula, *Chlorophytum capense*, *Campanula isophylla*, *Ipomoea* species, ivy-leaved and zonal pelargoniums, trailing *Lobelia erinus*, varieties of *Tradescantia fluminensis*, *Zebrina pendula*, *Mesembryanthemum criniflorum*, *Nepeta hederacea* and 'Gleam' nasturtiums (*Tropaeolum majus*). Keep the baskets indoors at night until all danger of frost is past.

☐ Deal with annual and perennial weed seedlings well before they flower and seed, either by hoeing or wetting their green top-growth with a paraquat/diquat contact weedkiller. Spot-treat the shoots of horsetails, bindweed, couch grass and plants of oxalis, lesser celandine, docks and ground elder with a systemic weedkiller or ammonium sulphamate solution.

THE VEGETABLE GARDEN

Make maincrop sowings of the frost-susceptible vegetables this month.

Runner beans should be sown 5cm (2in.) deep, 23cm (9in.) apart in double rows. Put two seeds at each station to allow for a low rate of germination and discard the weaker seedling if both emerge. Good varieties include 'Kelvedon Marvel' (1.2–1.5m (4–5ft)) for early cropping; and 'Achievement', 'Crusader', 'Enorma' and 'Prizewinner' (2–2.5m (7–8ft)).

Dwarf French beans should be sown 5cm (2in.) deep, 23–30cm (9–12in.) apart in rows 45cm (18in.) apart. Choose from 'Canadian Wonder', 'Kinghorn Wax', 'Loch Ness' and 'The Prince'.

Sow unusual vegetables such as asparagus pea, 45cm (18in.) tall, 'Sugar Pea', 1.5m (5ft) tall, 'Sugar Snap Pea', 1.5m (5ft) tall and petit pois 'Cobri' and 'Guillivert'. Be ready to give night frost protection to tender seedlings.

The main crop of beetroot should be sown to mature for winter store, placing seed capsules 2.5cm (1in.) deep, 7.5cm (3in.) apart, in rows 30cm (12in.) apart, removing weaker seedlings later. Use the long-rooted varieties 'Cheltenham', 'Cylindra' and 'Long Blood Red' on deep light soils and globe varieties 'Detroit', 'Ruddigore' and 'Burpees Golden' on ordinary and limy soils.

Sow turnips 'Snowball', 'Milan White' or 'Golden Perfection' for late summer use. Place seeds 1cm ($\frac{1}{2}$in.) deep, in rows 23cm (9in.) apart.

Continue successional sowings of lettuce, radishes and salad onion. See March notes for recommended varieties.

Continue sowings of seeds of sprouting broccoli ('Purple Sprouting', 'White Sprouting', 'Nine Star Perennial'), winter cabbage ('January King', 'Christmas Drumhead', 'Holland Late Winter') and cauliflowers ('English Winter', 'Walcheren Winter' strains, [Angers type, Nos. 1, 2, 3, 4, in southern and western regions]), 1cm ($\frac{1}{2}$in.) deep in a prepared seed-bed. Transplant the seedlings in late summer for overwintering and use next year.

☐ Plant out early Brussels sprouts, autumn cabbage and cauliflower sown in March for late summer and autumn harvest. Set with the first true leaves at soil level, firming in very well on ground well-manured for a previous crop, and limed in winter. Avoid planting on soil suspected of harbouring the club-root disease fungus.

☐ Thin carrot and onion seedlings to 10cm (4in.) apart. Do not leave discarded seedlings lying on the ground – they will attract pests. Refirm the soil around the remaining plant. Dust along the bases with a soil insecticide such as sevin or bromophos dust to prevent infestation from root fly larvae, in mid to late May.

☐ Plant out sweet corn seedlings raised under glass in late May. Choose a warm border, planting blocks of four, 23cm (9in.) apart, to ensure cross-pollination. Sweet corn can also be sown outdoors now, 2.5cm (1in.) deep, 23cm (9in.) apart in staggered double rows, 75cm (2ft 6in.) apart, in southern gardens and warm areas. Do not plant in long rows, but in squares, to aid pollination.

Thinning seedlings

THE FRUIT GARDEN

Spraying

Avoid using insecticides in the orchard when fruit bushes and
trees are in bloom, as pollinating bees and insects must have
safe access to ensure good crops.

Apples and pears. Catch late apples at the pink bud stage of
blossom development about the first week of May, and spray
with benomyl or captan to control fungus diseases such as scab
and mildew; and fenitrothion or thiophanate-methyl to control
aphids, caterpillars and insect pests. Choose a calm dry day,
preferably morning or afternoon (not noon or early evening),
and apply thoroughly to reach all surfaces of foliage and shoots.

Repeat the spraying when most of the petals (80 per cent or
more) have fallen. Use the fungicide only on pears, about mid-
May; but both fungicide and insecticide on apples, in late May,
to effect control of apple sawfly and red spider mites. Where
scab disease is very troublesome, chiefly in damp districts,
repeat the fungicidal application 3 weeks after petal fall.

Gooseberries. Spray bushes with systemic benomyl or thiram
or captan fungicide to control American mildew in about mid-
May; add a liquid derris insecticide to stop gooseberry sawfly
grubs defoliating a bush overnight.

Currants. Spray bushes with fenitrothion at the first open
flower and 3 weeks later for caterpillars, capsid bugs and black
currant gall mites.

Strawberries. Spray plants with a karathane or benomyl
systemic fungicide to control powdery mildew, and grey mould
(botrytis) diseases, about mid-May when the first flowers begin
to open; use liquid derris insecticide if aphids are seen.

Damsons and plums. Spray with derris, dimethoate and
formothion at the cot split stage of fruitlet formation, about the
third week of May, to control plum sawfly, winter moth
caterpillars and red spider mites.

☐ Cut out and burn cherry or plum shoots carrying dying
withered flowers and leaves. Cut back to clean healthy wood,
and paint or spray the cuts with a benomyl fungicidal solution.

☐ Keep a grassed-over orchard mown frequently, leaving the

fine clippings on the ground, but keeping the area around the tree bases free of grass. Feed with diluted liquid fertiliser in dry weather, applying as a foliar spray.

☐ Thin fruits on wall cherry, peach and plum trees as they form, at intervals during the month, allowing several leaves per fruit. Keep them well watered in dry weather; syringe to deter red spider mites.

☐ Weed the strawberry bed and mulch with straw, straw mats, peat, forestry bark or black sheet polythene when fruits begin to form, in late May or early June. In damp districts, trap slugs under halves of citrus fruit skins or put a slug bait down under the mulch.

THE ORNAMENTAL GARDEN

Hedges
Plant evergreen and coniferous hedges and screens with young plants with their roots in a soil ball; soak them overnight if dry. Plant in soil enriched with moist peat or compost and give a sprinkling of superphosphate to the roots. Firm in well, water in and overhead-spray on dry days. Minimise wind damage by placing temporary windbreaks of pea-sticks, chestnut paling, hurdles, netting or hessian on the windward side.

☐ Tip-prune growing points on hedges such as *Lonicera nitida* and privet (*Ligustrum* species) to induce branching low down; but leave leaders of conifers intact until they reach the height of the hedge desired.

Paths
Paths and driveways cleared of weed top-growth can be kept virtually weed-free for the summer by applying a dichlobenil residual herbicide.

Lawns
Mow established lawns more frequently as growth is made, but not too closely, in order to reduce the total amount of foliage removed in a season, while conserving grass vigour and soil fertility. Letting clippings return to the lawn may help to reduce moss and hold in moisture in hot weather, but is not pleasing to

the eye nor recommended if any flowering or seeding weeds or mosses are present.

☐ Cut new lawns when the leaves of grass reach about 5cm (2in.) high to half that height, using a well-sharpened mower or shears.

☐ If weed seedlings threaten to overwhelm the young grasses, apply an ioxynil selective weedkiller, specifically for new lawns. Hand-weed or spot-treat creeping perennial weeds. Continue cutting weekly, not closer than about 2cm ($\frac{3}{4}$in.).

☐ Start a chamomile lawn, if desired, during the growing season, from shoot cuttings of a non-flowering strain of *Chamaemelum nobile* syn. *Anthemis nobilis*, inserted about 10cm (4in.) apart in weed-free, levelled and firmed, light, sandy or chalky soil in open sun. This will give a ferny, scented sward that wears well and needs only occasional trimming to keep it within bounds.

The Rock Garden
Plant up now with dwarf evergreen shrubs and conifers if desired to provide permanent furnishing to the rock garden (see April notes). Water planting stations, and firm the soil and root-balls in well.

☐ Prepare a special seed-bed for the raising of alpine and rock garden plants from seeds. It should be well-drained by the liberal addition of coarse sand and grit, and enriched with sifted leaf-mould. Use only a dusting of superphosphate for fertiliser. Sow thinly with seeds of *Alyssum* species, *Aster alpinus*, *Aubrieta* hybrids, *Campanula carpatica*, *C. garganica*, *C. pusilla*, *Dianthus alpinus*, *D. deltoides*, *Erinus alpinus*, *Gentiana acaulis*, *G. septemfida*, *Gypsophila repens*, *Helianthemum nummularium*, *Iberis sempervirens*, *Primula* species, *Pulsatilla vulgaris*, mossy and encrusted saxifrage, *Sedum* species, *Silene schafta* and *Viola* species.

☐ Make provision for late summer and autumn colour by planting pot-grown late-flowering alpines – *Ceratostigma plumbaginoides*, *Cyananthus lobatus*, *C. microphyllus*, *Gentiana farreri*, *G.* 'Inverleith', *G.* 'Macaulay', varieties of *G. sino-ornata*, *Sedum spurium*, *S. cauticolum*, *Solidago virgaurea*, varities of *Daboecia cantabrica* and the bell heathers, *Erica cinerea*, which flower from summer into autumn.

☐ Layer low-growing shoots of shrubs such as *Andromeda polifolia* 'Nana' and winter flowering-heaths, by bending and bruising them gently and pegging down into the soil to root. Sever the rooted shoot from the parent plant next winter–spring and plant out.

Roses
Watch out for sucker shoots appearing. They usually have seven leaflets to a leaf, are very thorny, paler in colour than the main plant and grow rapidly. Catch them early, trace to their base, and wrench off rather than cut from the root, as cutting causes more suckers to sprout.

☐ Prevent infestation by the leaf-rolling sawfly by an application of a systemic insecticide about mid-May; check for aphids too.

Shrubs
Keep an eye on viburnums, especially *V. carlesii*, *V. opulus* and other deciduous species, and on the deciduous *Euonymus alatus* for aphids; counter immediately with derris, pyrethrum or malathion insecticide in spray or dust, before other plants are affected.

☐ If you are planning to move misplaced evergreen shrubs, do so early in this month, lifting with roots largely intact in the soil ball, and replanting at once in prepared stations. Long-established plants move least successfully, unless they can be lifted with roots and soil undisturbed.

☐ Finish planting new evergreen shrubs before mid-May. Water with dilute feed (seaweed extracts are excellent) in a band around the soil ball to get roots growing into the surrounding soil.

☐ Plant bamboos now if desired in reasonably moist soils, but choose carefully: many varieties sucker and spread insidiously. Look to *Arundinaria* (syn. *Semiarundinaria*) *fastuosa* for a tall hedge or group; *A. murielae* for elegance; *A. nitida* for ornamental clumps; *Phyllostachys flexuosa* and *P. nigra*, with its varieties, both have graceful slender canes.

☐ Prune wall-growing japonica (*Chaenomeles speciosa*), reducing flowered lateral shoots by a half to two-thirds.

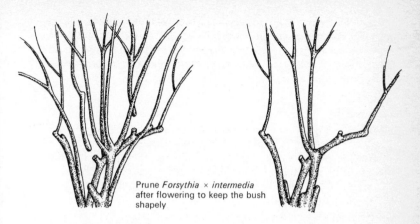

Prune *Forsythia × intermedia* after flowering to keep the bush shapely

☐ Prune forsythias as the flowers fade. Cut out entirely a proportion of the flowered and older stems of *F. × intermedia* annually to preserve the shapeliness of the shrubs; leave most of the young unflowered shoots intact. Prune *F. suspensa* by cutting lateral flowered shoots back near to their base. Prune *F. ovata* lightly, or not at all.

☐ Cut out a few shoots of the oldest wood of flowering currant (*Ribes sanguineum*), spent older shoots of *Spiraea × arguta*, leggy shoots of *Mahonia aquifolium*, the older wood of *Kerria japonica*, and dead or weakly shoots on all shrubs. As a rule, however, shrubs that are suited to their positions and growing healthily need no pruning except to keep them to shape and within bounds.

Trees

Wrap stems of newly planted trees in plastic guards or gaiters if rabbits or hares are likely to invade the garden.

☐ Finish planting out evergreen trees and conifers, watering well, and keeping them syringed or sprayed from overhead on dry days.

☐ Check for dead snags, cavities and cankers in established trees, and, if present, cut back rotten wood to firm healthy tissue. Paint the cuts with a bituminous tree paint. Fill in large cavities with cold bituminous asphalt, smoothing to a flush finish to shed rain.

☐ Do not prune flowering or ornamental trees without good reason; it is not necessary when growth is healthy, though some need time to settle down to a flowering rhythm. However do dead-head where possible such trees as lilac otherwise the faded flowers remain all summer.

The Water Garden

Planting. This is the month to plant aquatic and bog plants when the weather is congenial. Aim to provide a balance of surface-leafing aquatics like water lilies, underwater oxygenating plants, and free-living, top-of-the-water plants in pools.

Select water lilies, *Nymphaea* species, for colour and to suit the depth of the pool:

Planting depth 30–45cm (12–18in.)
> *N. candida,* white
> *N. pygmaea alba,* snow-white
> *N. 'Helvola',* pale primrose

Planting depth 45–60cm (18in–2ft)
> *N.* × *laydekeri* 'Purpurata', deep pink
> *N.* × *laydekeri* 'Lilacea', rosy-lilac
> *N.* × 'Froebelii', wine-red
> *N.* × 'Escarboucle', brilliant red
> *N.* × 'Mme Wilfron Gonnère', rich pink
> *N.* × 'James Brydon', deep rosy-pink
> *N.* × *marliacea* 'Chromatella', soft yellow
> *N.* × *m.* 'Carnea', pink fading to white
> *N.* × *m.* 'Rosea', pale pink

Planting depth 1m (39in.) or more
> *N. tuberosa* 'Rosea', pink
> *N. alba,* white
> *N.* × 'Colossea', blush pink changing to white
> *N.* × 'Gladstoniana', white

Also useful for shade-bearing, surface-floating leaves are the water hawthorn (*Aponogeton distachyus*) for water 23–60cm (9in–2ft) deep; and the spatterdock (*Nuphar advena*) for water up to 60cm (2ft) deep. The water fringe, *Nymphoides peltata*, is good for shallow waters. The water violet, *Hottonia palustris*, is an oxygenating plant for shallow (up to 25cm (10in.)) pools.

☐ Keep plants damp, especially at their roots, until the moment of planting. Plant water lilies and oxygenating plants directly in bottom soil. Special aquatic baskets, boxes, or plastic crates, filled with good fibrous loam, are more convenient for water lilies; for planting in deep water place them on raised brickwork pedestals at the level at which the plants grow best.

Plant underwater oxygenating specimens from May to early September, using rooted plants or cuttings inserted in soil and weighted so that they sink to the bottom. Useful species are *Elodea canadensis, E. crispa, Potamogeton densus, P. crispus* and *Ranunculus aquatilis.*

Fill new or renovated pools gradually. At first, just cover newly planted stock, then add water gradually at 2- to 4-day intervals as the temperature adjusts to 15.5°C (60°F) or more. When the pool is full, introduce a few floating plants such as *Azolla caroliniana, Hydrocharis morsus-ranae* and *Stratiotes aloides.*

Allow a few weeks for the pool and plants to settle before introducing fish. Balanced planting ensures clear, healthy water.

This is the best time to plant marginal waters with aquatic plants, and damp, wet, boggy ground with moisture-loving plants, though they are available for planting right up to October.

☐ Lift, divide and replant overcrowded aquatic plants this month. Cut away the older thick bare rhizomatous roots of water lilies, and replant the rootstock and crowns. Most underwater oxygenators can be lifted as they age and new plants propagated from cuttings or by simple division. This is necessary from time to time to avoid a pool becoming too thickly populated with stems and shoots. Lift old clumps of marginal and aquatic bog plants for division in May or after flowering.

THE GARDEN UNDER GLASS

Remove cloches from crops and plants sown earlier in the year as the danger of night frosts recedes, or temperatures may go too high. Remove protection from frost-susceptible crops in the daytime only. This is the month when cloches which can be ventilated prove really worth while.

☐ Prepare cold frames for growing cucumbers 'Conqueror' or 'Fertila F₁; melons 'Charentais', 'Ogen', 'Sweetheart', and

'Tiger'; or grow under barn cloches. Keep well watered throughout the growing season. Ventilate freely on hot days.

☐ Harden off in a cold frame bedding plants, annuals, vegetable seedlings and tomato plants and cucumbers intended for outdoor cropping. Shade them from hot sun and keep well watered and ventilated.

☐ Line the base of a deep frame on a hard surface such as concrete with capillary matting, when it is being used to house pot plants such as chrysanthemums or carnations, to prevent them drying out.

☐ Keep pests such as ants, slugs, snails and woodlice out of frames with a dusting of a pirimiphos-methyl powder, and a band of 8 parts volume hydrated lime to 1 part powdered alum around the external base of the frames.

The Cool Greenhouse
Continue to sow seeds if wanted: cineraria (*Senecio cruentus* hybrids) should be sown shallowly in pots or pans of seed compost, at 13–15°C (55–60°F), for winter flowering. Keep moist and shaded from hot sun. *Stellata* hybrids give large plants; *Multiflora nana* strains give compact specimens. All provide beautiful winter colour.

Herbaceous strains of calceolaria should be placed on the compost surface, in glass-covered pans at 18°C (65°F), for flowering next spring.

Celosia argentea cristata (cockscombs), *C. a. plumosa* (Prince of Wales' feathers) and *Celsia arcturus* (Cretan mullein) should be sown at a temperature of about 18°C (65°F) for late summer/autumn bloom.

☐ Snap off the spent flowerheads of bulbous and cormous indoor plants (daffodils, tulips, hyacinths) and replant them intact out of doors, giving a liquid feed. When the leaves die lift and sort them for replanting out of doors.

☐ Stop young chrysanthemum plants in pots when 15–23cm (6–9in.) high, pinching out the growing point. Place the pots outdoors in the latter half of the month, in a wind-sheltered spot, on a layer of ashes, sheet polythene or boards. Stake the plants and water them daily if necessary.

☐ Plant cucumber plants in the greenhouse border when night

temperatures are unlikely to fall below 15.5°C (60°F), and when they can be given the humid conditions they require, separate from tomatoes. To grow with tomatoes, under similar conditions, plant the variety 'Conqueror'.

Pot on rooted cuttings of zonal pelargoniums intended for winter flowering; place outdoors in sheltered warm border later, and remove early flowers.

☐ Disbud apricots, nectarines, and peaches throughout the month. Nip off the tip growth of new shoots coming from wood buds from which extension is not wanted. Select a replacement shoot from near the base of the current bearing shoot to grow out and become the new fruit-bearing shoot. Stop it when about 60cm (2ft) long, by pinching out the tip, subsequently stopping any laterals at the first leaf. Syringe fruit trees under glass on warm, sunny days.

☐ Move out pot-growing fruit trees to wind-sheltered sunny positions when the fruits have set and keep well watered.

☐ Start thinning bunches of grapes as soon as fruitlets form, removing those crowding the centre first, and then the outer ones, in order to give the remaining fruits ample space in which to develop. Allow only one bunch on each lateral shoot. Prune each lateral at the second leaf beyond the bunch of fruit.

☐ Take cuttings of young, non-flowered shoots, 5–7.5cm (2–3in.) long, of such plants as Cape heaths (*Erica canaliculata*), winter- and spring-flowering heaths (*Erica herbacea*, *E. erigena*), and the related *Epacris* species. Insert in a cuttings compost in deep pans. Keep them moist and shaded from hot sun.

☐ Put down capillary matting which must be kept permanently moist, on greenhouse benches to minimise watering time. This system is excellent for pot plants. From time to time add an algaecide to the water to prevent greening.

☐ Be ready to combat attacks by diseases and pests in their early stages with appropriate fungicides and insecticides. To apply these substances evenly, thoroughly and most economically, use a fine mist sprayer or aerosol. A systemic fungicide is invaluable for flowering and food plants in early stages of growth. Read the manufacturer's instructions before using insecticides. Derris- and pyrethrum-based insecticides are the safest to use on food crops near harvest.

P.T.O.

Yellow berberis – prune unwanted branches immediately after flowering, if necessary.

Erica carnea heathers – trim lightly as soon as flowers have faded. Prune back straggly shoots, but do not cut into old wood.

Hebe – cut back straggly shoots. Remove frost-damaged branches.

Holly – trim if necessary. Remove all-green branches. (Needs sun for variegation).

Flame of the forest – remove dead flowers.

June

Some June plants in flower and vegetables in season

(As the majority of flowers listed continue into July, those that have a short June season only are marked with *)

The Flower Garden

Aethionema
Achillea
Alchemilla
Allium
Alstroemeria
Alyssum
Anaphalis
Anchusa
Aquilegia
Armeria
Asperula
Asphodel lily
Astrantia
Aubrieta
Ballota
Baptisia
Camassia
Campanula
Coreopsis
Cornflower
Crepis
Dianthus
Delphinium
Echinops (globe thistle)
Edelweiss
Erigeron (fleabane)
Euphorbia
Gaillardia
Geum
Geranium
Globe daisy
Gypsophila
Hemerocallis (day lily)
Heucera
Hosta
Inula
Iris
Limonium (sea lavender)
Lily of the valley
Linum (flax)
Lupin
Lychnis (campion)
Mallow (lavatera)
Meconopsis
Nierembergia
Oenthera (evening primrose)
Pansy
Penstemon
Phlomis
Phlox
Polemonium (Jacob's ladder)
Polygonum
Potentilla
Primula
Pyrethrum
Ranunculus (buttercup)
Salvia
Scabious
Sedum
Sempervivum
Sidalcea
Shamrock
Sisyrinchium*
Stachys (lamb's ears)
Thalictrum (meadow rue)
Thyme
Tiarella
Verbascum
Veronica

The Ornamental Garden

Abelia*
Buddleia*
Broom
Cistus*
Clematis
Cornus kousa
Cotoneaster*
Cytisus
Daphne
Deutzia
Escallonia
False acacia (Robinia)
Fuchsia
Hawthorn*
Hebe
Honeysuckle
Hypericum (St John's Wort)
Laburnum*
Lilac (syringa)*
Magnolia
Olearia
Passion flower
Pyracantha
Philadelphus
Rhododendrons*
Roses
Rubus
Santolina
Senecio greyii
Spirea
Viburnum
Weigela*

Water Garden
Marsh marigold

Vegetables in season

Asparagus
Beans, broad
Broccoli
Cabbage (spring)
Lettuce
Onion (salad)
Peas
Potatoes
Radish
Spinach

Fruit in season

Gooseberry
Rhubarb
Strawberry

The garden comes into its own in June, and apart from watching everything grow and blossom, keeping the weeds at bay and watering if necessary are the most time-consuming occupations this month.

Watering. Water if possible *before* the plants show signs of flagging or wilting, and aim to soak the soil rather than merely wet the surface. Again, if possible, let the water fall like rain through the air, gathering oxygen and a little warmth; the finer the spray, the better the effect. Water in the cooler morning and evening hours of the day to make every drop count. If the use of a hose, sprinkler or overhead irrigation is banned and the watering can must be used, add a little soluble fertiliser to make the water go further in meeting plant needs. Ordinary domestic waste water from bathroom or kitchen can usually be used – let it stand for 24 hours to settle and use the clearer top water.

☐ Make good use of mulches to cut down moisture losses from the soil and to keep down weeds. A mulch is a top-dressing of organic materials (compost, moist peat, pulverised bark, weathered sawdust, chopped straw, newspaper, lawn clippings (provided no weed-killer has been used recently), black sheet polythene, even chippings or gravel for rock plants). Place it over the rooting area of plants, under branches, stems or spread of leaves, leaving the area round the base bare. Apply when the soil is moist, after rain or watering. Renew when necessary.

THE FLOWER GARDEN

Keep an eye on annuals and water in the early morning or evening in dry weather. Hardy annuals coming into flower this month should include anchusa, bartonia, candytuft (*Iberis*), Californian poppy (*eschscholzia*), gypsophila, larkspur (*Delphinium ajacis*), toadflax (*Linaria*), poppy, night-scented stock (*Matthiola bicornis*), morning glory (*Convolvulus major* syn. *Ipomaea purpurea*), love-in-a-mist (*Nigella damascena*), and Virginian stock (*Malcolmia maritima*). Among half-hardy annuals quick off the mark are ageratum, African marigold, French marigold, lobelia, mesembryanthemum, nasturtium, nicotiana, petunia and verbena; and biennials such as Canterbury bells, stocks and sweet william. To keep them flowering from June to September, dead-head frequently.

☐ There is still time to plant gladioli corms, dahlias and begonias, which do well in partial shade.

☐ Thin sowings of outdoor annuals as soon as the plants can be grasped between finger and thumb.

☐ Complete planting out of annuals to furnish bedding schemes or fill empty spaces in borders or rock gardens early in the month. If the soil is dry, soak it a few hours before planting.

☐ Shade from hot direct sun can be life-saving for plants in sandy, chalky, stony soils, and one of the quickest and best ways to provide it is to sow quick-growing annuals such as morning glory, nasturtiums and sunflowers in beds and borders trained on wigwams of sticks or canes and string. Shade newly planted perennials and shrubs with small-mesh green plastic netting in hot weather.

☐ When the foliage dies lift clumps of corms and bulbs which gave few flowers, or are overcrowded; sort through them and reserve the largest bulbs for flowering next year. Discard any that are damaged, soft or mushy. Smaller offset bulbs and corms will need to be planted on reserve ground to grow on for one or two years.

☐ Propagate *Dianthus* (border carnations) towards the end of the month and in July by taking 'pipings' – ends of unflowered young shoots with 3 or 4 pairs of leaves, detached by giving a gentle pull at the nodes. Remove the lowest pair of leaves and insert the shoots in porous soil under a cloche or in pots in a cold frame.

Disbud axillary buds of border carnations when they can be rubbed off easily, to encourage large single blooms.

THE VEGETABLE GARDEN

Sowing. Continue to sow the following:

French beans and runner beans can be sown this month and up until early July in the south.

Savoy cabbage ('January King', 'January Queen'); and cabbage ('Winter Monarch') for next spring's crop.

Carrots 'Chantenay Early Red Core' and 'Early Nantes' for autumn crops.

Successional sowing of lettuce ('All the Year Round', 'Arctic

King', 'Avondefiance', 'Winter Density', 'Little Gem'), salad onion ('White Lisbon') and turnip ('Snowball').

Endive ('Green Batavian') for unusual winter salads.

Parsley thinly on humus-rich soil after rain. Dress the seeds with bone flour and allow at least 4 weeks for germination.

☐ Plant out celery and leeks up to mid July; make plantings of sprouting broccoli, winter Brussels sprouts, autumn cauliflower and savoy cabbages this month and next. Dip the roots of brassicas in a solution of a benomyl systemic fungicide to guard against club root disease.

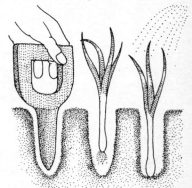

☐ Plant outdoor tomatoes ('Outdoor Girl', 'The Amateur' for bush plants;

Use a dibber to plant out leek seedlings and water in well

'Alicante', 'Harbinger' for tall plants) this month in a warm sheltered sunny position when all danger of frost is past.

☐ Stop cutting asparagus by 21 June. Weed the bed by hoe or by applying a paraquat/diquat contact herbicide; and rake in a dressing of a compound vegetable fertiliser at 250g/m² (8oz per sq. yd), to encourage strong growth next year.

☐ Prune out the shoot tips of broad beans at the first sign of blackfly aphids to prevent severe infestation of all plants. Water with a very diluted solution of potassium nitrate half a teaspoon to 5 litres (1 gallon) from overhead. This makes the plants distasteful to the pests and benefits growth – a fillip for most plants coming under attack from greenfly or blackfly.

THE FRUIT GARDEN

Net strawberries and bush fruits not grown in a fruit cage for protection against birds.

☐ Thin gooseberry fruits when they reach marble size.
Use them for cooking and let the rest grow on to dessert size.

☐ Thin fruits on pear trees about mid-June to 2 or 3 fruits per cluster, to a single fruit on young trees or trees with only moderate foliage. The more leaves, the bigger the crop that can be carried.

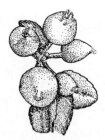

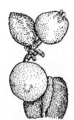

Thin apples to leave one or two healthy fruits per truss

☐ Thin apples after the 'June Drop', when small embryo fruits are shed naturally. Thin early-ripening culinary varieties first to 2 or 3 apples per cluster; remove the short-stalked 'king' apple central to the cluster first. For extra-large fruits, especially on varieties such as 'Grenadier', 'Monarch', 'Newton Wonder', 'Rev. W. Wilks' and 'Charles Ross', reduce clusters to single apples, well-spaced on the branches. Thin dessert apples about the last week in the month, to singles or pairs, to be sure of large fruits.

☐ Repeat petal-fall sprays on neglected pear and apple trees when fruitlets are pea-size (about the second to third week of the month) to reinforce protection against scab and mildew.

☐ Spray apples and pears against codling moth infestation with derris or malathion in latter half of the month, and be ensured of fewer maggoty fruits at harvest-time.

☐ Keep a close watch on pear trees in the south and midlands which show wilting and browning blossom clusters. If this progresses to cankering of spurs and branches, the darkening leaves hanging on shoots that look as if they have been scorched by fire, fire blight may be to blame. This highly infectious bacterial disease must be reported to the Ministry of Agriculture. Affected trees must be destroyed.

☐ Continue to mow grass under fruit trees, letting the cuttings return to the soil. Give a light dressing of Chilean potash nitrate to speed their decomposition and benefit the trees.

☐ Examine forming raspberry fruits late in the month for greyish depressed druplets and the presence of tiny white grubs – signs of infestation by the raspberry beetle. If present spray or dust with a derris insecticide.

☐ Check forming fruits of strawberries and soft fruits for the formation of a grey fluffy mould (botrytis) in damp weather, especially on plants under netting. Pick off seriously infected fruits and burn. Prevention lies in spraying with a systemic fungicide, such as benomyl, just before flowering.

THE ORNAMENTAL GARDEN

Hedges
Prune informal spring-flowering hedges – *Berberis darwinii*, *B.* × *stenophylla*, forsythia, flowering currant, pyracantha, *Spiraea arguta*, *S. thunbergii* and *Viburnum tinus* – trimming flowered shoots back to within a few buds or leaves of their base.

☐ Trim fast-growing hedges – *Lonicera nitida*, privet, thorn, myrobalan and flowering plum – with the sides parallel or tapering to the top and repeat in 3–4 weeks for a close-knit hedge.

Paths
Continue to keep weeds down by spot-treatment. Use a selective lawn weedkiller for broad-leaved weeds and a dalapon weedkiller for grasses. If using a total weedkiller be sure to restrict application to the weeds.

Lawns
Continue to mow frequently, cutting higher in dry weather.
Give a supplementary feed in mid-June, before or just after rain. Better still apply a dilute liquid solution, if the weather is dry.
In dry weather or drought, do not apply selective weedkillers, which may check grass growth, or lawn sand, which will burn the grasses.

Anticipate drought by slitting or spiking the turf, and watering to soak – treat one area at a time, if the period for watering is restricted; well-soaked, the lawn can continue growing for some weeks.

Compost lawn mowings treated with any weedkiller separately. They will be safe for use after 3–4 months' decomposition.

The Rock Garden

☐ Increase early-flowering saxifrages (from the engleria group) leaves and crown buds (such as *Primula denticulata*) by lifting, dividing and replanting immediately in damp weather; or pot in peat-wood fibre pots, and place in a shady cold frame for planting out in late summer or autumn.

☐ Increase early-flowering saxifrages (from the Engleria group) by detaching single rosettes of the encrusted silvery leaves, with stem, and inserting in porous loam in partial shade, to root.

☐ Every third or fourth year, lift dwarf corms and bulbs such as crocus, narcissus, puschkinia and scilla, when the leaves die down. Discard damaged or spent specimens. Replant the healthy ones at once and place bulblets or offsets in a nursery bed to grow on.

☐ Fill empty spaces now showing on rock terraces with dwarf annuals for summer colour, firming into moist soil.

Roses

Keep growth vigorous by watering very freely, wetting the soil several inches down at the first onset of a dry spell; give a foliar feed a week later and keep the beds well mulched.

☐ Inspect for powdery mildew infection – white, powdery fungal deposit on leaves – when warm days follow cool, dewy nights, and control with a systemic fungicide such as dinocap or mildothane. Repeat the treatment 2 weeks later.

☐ Look out for purplish-black patches on the leaves caused by blackspot fungus when the weather becomes cool and damp. The spores are airborne from last year's shoots and fallen leaves, not the soil. Contain with a systemic, dinocap, captan, thiram or copper fungicide.

☐ Keep a keen look-out for pests, which are apt to increase

rapidly in close-planted rose beds. Detach rolled-in leaflets and leaves, indicating the presence of sawfly or tortrix moth caterpillars; partially eaten flower buds, usually consumed by chafers, and skeletonised leaves, eaten by rose slugworms. Apply an insecticide and repeat as needed. When leaves are being eaten look for caterpillars, especially loopers or geometers, which arch as they walk, and pick them off. Semi-circular fragments scalloped out of the leaves probably mean that leaf-cutter bees are at work. There is no easy control, but the damage is seldom very serious.

☐ Look for red spider mites on the undersides of leaves if they become mottled, dry and yellow, falling prematurely. They are a particular problem in hot weather and dry conditions, particularly on wall-grown roses and are best controlled with a systemic insecticide, or derris, malathion or pyrethrum applied to cover above and below leaf surfaces.

☐ Cut blooms with care; prune cleanly above buds on the stems that will give new growth in an outward direction. Cut in the early morning or late evening, slit the stem and immerse in water for a few hours before arranging. Remove damaged and spent flowerheads promptly to a healthy leaf. Rake in a dressing of a complete rose fertiliser at about a third of the normal application, after the first flush of flowers is over.

Shrubs
Prune spring-flowering shrubs – those that flower chiefly on the previous year's shoots – as their blooms fade, when it is essential to shape their habit or encourage new young growth by cutting away part of the old. A shrub that is healthy and has space for expansion, needs little or no pruning except to remove faded blooms. On shrubs such as lilacs and rhododendrons (including azaleas), simply cut out spent flowerheads, rather than let them waste energy on seed formation. Twist off rather than cutting, taking great care not to damage the new buds already forming below the faded flowers.

☐ Be discriminating about planting out this month. Do not plant bare-rooted shrubs (or trees), now starting to grow; even if they survive they will be handicapped. If it is essential to plant this month or at any time during the summer, use young healthy container-grown specimens, not overgrown 'bargains' which have been in their pots for too long. Prepare the planting station well, breaking up the base, water thoroughly, place the container in the hole and then remove it. Pack around with good soil containing up to 50 per cent of moist peat, pulverised bark, organic compost, and a good sprinkling of hoof and horn and bone meal, to entice roots to grow from the container-bound rootstock; firm and finally water again.

☐ Keep newly planted evergreens watered and mulched.

☐ Watch for suckers appearing from the rootstocks of grafted plants such as flowering quinces, lilacs, and flowering almonds, cherries, and peaches of the *Prunus* genus. Detach them at base.

Trees
Prune if necessary to shape ornamental trees of the *Prunus* genus, such as almonds, cherries, peaches and plums as they come fully into leaf this month. Thin shoots and cut out overhanging or unwanted branches to minimise the loss of sap in bleeding, and to avoid silver leaf fungus infection. Trees such as birches, maples and walnuts are best pruned now when in full leaf to prevent bleeding. Dress cut surfaces with a tree antiseptic or fungicidal solution.

☐ Overhead-water newly planted trees in dry periods, especially evergreens and conifers.

☐ Keep down weeds, especially couch grass, in the rooting area of young trees. Couch grass is inhibitory to the roots of other plants below ground, but can be checked with a dalapon weedkiller.

The Water Garden
Stop the greening of water in pools without fish by introducing a stock of live daphnia (from aquarium shops). This is more effective than changing the water, though the natural cure is balanced planting (see May notes).

☐ Remove blanketweed, flannelweed, or silkweed, which are filamentous growths of algae, by drawing netting over the surface or inserting a forked stick and gathering the weed by turning it round and round. Algae are not directly harmful to fish or plants but unsightly. An algaecide which is harmless to fish and plants may be used on a still evening.

☐ Replace water lost by evaporation in hot weather with water at the same temperature as that in the pool. Wash into the pool any blackfly aphids seen on plant leaves by a gentle hosing, if the pool is stocked with fish which feed on aphids.

☐ Introduce fish during summer months when plants are making good growth and the water is settled and clear. Place their container on the surface of the water and leave it for an hour to attune to the water's temperature before releasing the fish.

☐ Bear in mind that most insecticides and some fungicides are toxic to fish; do not use them near a pool unless they are safe for water.

☐ Watch out for great diving beetles, silver diving beetles and their larvae; dragonfly naiads, water boatmen, water stick insects, water scorpions and leeches in the water. All these are harmful to fish. Have a small mesh scoop or strainer to hand with which to catch them. The fish themselves will keep the pool low in mosquitoes and caddis flies.

THE GARDEN UNDER GLASS

Ventilate plants in frames freely. For the next 12 to 14 weeks, frame lights may be fully open or left off, except on days and nights when weather protection is needed. Have lath frames, green-shading polythene sheeting or small mesh plastic netting at hand to put over on hot days.

Keep frames open in hot weather

☐ As cloche-grown crops and flowers mature and are harvested, clean the cloches and overhaul them for autumn use.

Greenhouse Gardening
Overhaul heating apparatus and systems in the cool greenhouse during the warm months. There is little difference in the management of cold or cool greenhouses until September.

☐ Aim to keep temperatures within the range of 15.5°C (60°F) at night and up to 24–27°C (75–80°F) at midday, by ventilating freely as temperatures rise. Keep humidity buoyant by damping

115

down – watering paths, stages, and interiors on hot days, especially in the mornings; spray plants and increase water supplies as growth flourishes.

☐ Give shade during the heat of the day, using a method that can be adjusted to needs: blinds, lath frames or tinted plastic sheeting. For semi-permanent shade in southern and well-sunned exposures, proprietary washes can be applied to the glass. A fluid paste of flour and water serves the purpose and can easily be removed in autumn. Automatic shading systems are also available.

☐ Dry off bulbous plants which have flowered by withholding water as leaves begin to wither. Store under staging or in sheds.

☐ Transfer spring-potted or early-flowering shrubs, now over, to outdoor quarters in a warm sheltered position with partial shade. Keep regularly watered, with occasional liquid feed, until autumn.

☐ Stop decorative chrysanthemums a second time in mid to late June, if a high yield of blooms is required. Exhibition plants do need this second stopping to give exceptional but fewer blooms. Stake the plants.

☐ Liquid feed perpetual-flowering carnations now coming into bud.

☐ Syringe cucumbers now growing freely each morning and shade from hot sun. Stop the main stem when tall enough, at the 4 or 5ft wire, and train and fasten laterals to supporting wires to carry the fruits.

☐ Mist-spray flower clusters (trusses) on tomato plants when fully open in the morning to ensure fruit-setting. Avoid any hiatus in watering in order to prevent such troubles as dry-set and blossom-end rot. Water regularly, adjusting the quantity according to weather conditions and light intensity – giving less when the temperature drops and cloud is prevalent. Give balanced liquid feeds in step with fruit formation and growth. Remove side-shoots from leaf axils cleanly, as soon as they form.

☐ Complete the thinning of fruitlets on grapes, and stop the growth of secondary lateral shoots just beyond their second leaves.

☐ Keep fruit tree borders and fruits in pots well watered; trickle watering is labour-saving and invaluable.

☐ Sow seeds of *Gerbera jamesonii* and hybrids to give perennial pot plants for flowering next year in a cool greenhouse.

Sow seeds of the Cape primrose (*Streptocarpus*) at 18–21°C (65–70°F) to give plants to come into flower for indoors next spring.

Sow fresh seeds of *Primula obconica*, *P. kewensis*, *P. sinensis* and *P. malacoides* to provide flowering pot plants for winter and spring.

☐ Propagate greenhouse shrubs, such as abutilon, acacia, clethra, epacris, erica and fuchsia from half-ripe, partially mature, firm side shoots as they are available. Detach with a small heel or sliver of older wood. Insert in deep pans or pots of potting compost and keep moist in partial shade until rooting has taken place.

Propagate *Camellia japonica* and its varieties from leaf cuttings. Select single young firm leaves, taken with basal bud and a small supporting piece of branch wood. Insert them in lime-free porous compost and provide a warm humid atmosphere; enclose the pots in plastic bags, with a few holes punched for ventilation, or preferably root in a propagating unit with mist-spray conditions.

☐ Hand-pollinate melons, when there are 6 or so female flowers (those with a small roundish swelling behind the petals), by gently pressing a male flower (with pollen-bearing stamens), petals held back, into their faces, at about midday on a warm sunny day. When fruits begin to swell, reduce numbers to not more than 4 per plant, and pinch out any subsequent flowers.

Alyssum saxatile (yellow) — trim stems back once the flowers have faded.

Aubrieta — cut back after flowering finished.

Iberis — Dead head regularly.

Pyracanthus — cut back unwanted shoots immediately after flowering.

Helianthemums — dead head regularly.

117

July

Some July plants in flower and vegetables in season

See also the June list for the many plants flowering from June to August. The following appear this month:

The Flower Garden

Acaena
Acanthus
Aconitum
Agapanthus
Antirrhinum
Astilbe
Calceolaria
Cephalaria
Cimicifuga
Cornflower
Crinum
Cynara (globe artichoke)
Dahlia
Dimorphotheca
Helenium
Helichrysum
Hollyhock
Ligularia (ragwort)
Lysimachia (yellow loose-strife)
Lythrum (purple loose-strife)
Lily
Lobelia
Mallow
Mesembryanthemum
Morning glory
Nasturtium
Petunia
Phlox
Phygelius (cape figwort)
Physostegia
Polygonum
Red hot poker
Rodgersia

Roses
Rudbeckia
Salvia
Sedum
Stachys (lamb's ears)
Sea lavender
Stock
Stokesia
Sweet pea
Tobacco plant
Tunica
Veratrum
Verbascum
Verbena
Veronica

The Ornamental Garden

Buddleia
Catalpa
Clematis × jackmanii (large flowered hybrids)
Escallonia
Eucryphia
Fuchsia
Hebe
Hydrangea
Hypericum
Jasmine
Lavender
Passion flower

Vegetables in season

Artichoke, globe
Beans, broad, dwarf, French, runner
Beetroot
Carrots
Cucumber
Lettuce
Marrow
Peas
Potatoes
Radish
Spinach

Fruit in season

Black currant
Gooseberry
Raspberry
Red currant
Strawberry

If the warm summer days are not too dry, even masochistic gardeners should be able to enjoy the fruits of their labours and relax.

Compost. A compost heap started now and carefully managed will be ready for use when digging in the early winter. This means gathering and economically and efficiently rotting down the organic and plant waste of garden and home into humus-forming manure. Raw materials are organic animal and plant residues, soft plant stems, leaves, lawn mowings, soft prunings, spent flowers, discarded leaves and stems of crops,

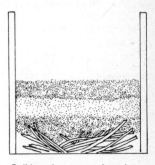

Build up the compost heap in layers

hay, straw, shredded newspaper, kitchen waste, crushed eggshells, wool, even sawdust – but not flowering or seeding weeds, tough perennial weed roots, diseased plants, woody plants or prunings, man-made fibres, plastic or metal.

Build the heap square in shape. A 1.5m (5ft) cube is a good size to aim for in most gardens. Make a container of wire netting attached to corner posts, or use one of the ready-made compost bins. It is important to admit enough air all around the heap. Build it up in layers at least 15cm (6in.) deep, preferably 30cm (12in.). Water each layer well and treat with an activator to speed up the process of decomposition. Use a proprietary substance according to the manufacturer's instructions or sulphate of ammonia at 15g ($\frac{1}{2}$oz) per layer. Put a thin layer of weed-free soil on top. The occasional addition of a handful of hydrated garden lime is useful in gardens where the soil is acid, but should not be used in conjunction with sulphate of ammonia. Turning the heap sides to middle speeds decomposition but is not essential. If it is turned, slight moisture loss will occur, so compensate with a light watering. Once the heap has reached the right height, cover it with a final layer of soil. It will heat up as decomposition proceeds. After about 12 weeks, rather longer in cold weather, the heap should have turned into a dark, soft, crumbly, sweet-smelling material for digging into the vegetable patch or spreading as a nourishing mulch in the ornamental garden.

THE FLOWER GARDEN

Ensure that late-flowering border plants such as Michaelmas daisies, solidago, heleniums, phlox and other tall plants are securely staked.

Dead-head annuals and border plants to encourage fresh buds and flowers.

Stop earwigs ascending dahlia plants by dusting around the base with a sevin or gamma-HCH insecticidal powder.

☐ Lift tulip bulbs as their foliage fades. Dry them off in an airy shady place, and sort through them for replanting in October–November. Discard and burn any bulbs showing signs of tulip fire – rotten tissue and black fungus-bearing spores. Dust healthy bulbs with thiram before storing.

☐ Lift and divide old clumps of bearded irises as soon as flowering is over, replanting the younger rhizomes and roots immediately in moist, organically enriched soil. In dry weather, however, leave the plants alone until autumn.

☐ Plant the corms of the autumn crocus, *Colchicum autumnale*, *C. speciosum*, and their varieties and hybrids, as soon as available. Place them 10–15cm (4–6in.) deep in any well-drained soil, in areas where their bulky, leek-like foliage which appears in spring can be accommodated and allowed unrestricted growth.

Plant the corms of true autumn-flowering crocuses such as *Crocus asturicus*, *C. byzantinus*, *C. cancellatus*, *C. kotschyanus*, *C. longiflorus*, *C. medius*, *C. ochroleucus*, *C. pulchellus*, and *C. speciosus*, about 7.5cm (3in.) deep, in well-drained soil in borders, rock gardens or shrubberies.

☐ Propagate border carnations by layering. Choose young, non-flower-bearing shoots lying near the ground. Make a slanting cut half-way through a node, and peg this part down. Mound good soil compost over it and leave it to root. Sever from the parent plant and plant out in autumn.

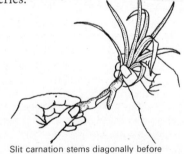

Slit carnation stems diagonally before layering

☐ Plant the tubers of autumn-flowering cyclamen, *Cyclamen cilicium*, *C. europaeum*, and *C. neapolitanum*, 2.5–5cm (1–2in.) deep in humus-rich soil, lightly limed, where they can be left undisturbed in partial shade.

☐ Thin and/or transplant seedlings of biennials and spring-sown perennials prior to final autumn planting-out.

☐ Prevent mildews with an application of systemic fungicide.

THE VEGETABLE GARDEN

Lift early varieties of potatoes as needed, or when top growth begins to yellow. After raking, and giving a light dressing of a complete fertiliser, sow the ground with lettuce, quick-maturing carrot ('Nantes'), turnip ('Golden Ball'), round beet, cabbage ('Harbinger', 'Wheeler's Imperial'); or, in the north, 'Hungry Gap' kale.

Earth up maincrop potatoes for the last time; in areas vulnerable to blight, spray with a preventive fungicide such as liquid copper, Bordeaux mixture, or benomyl: early July in the south-west; mid-July in the midlands and the north. Repeat 2 weeks later to protect new growth.

☐ Lift garlic and shallot bulbs as the tops turn yellow. Choose a fine day; dry out of the sun, and store in a cool shed.

☐ Plant out seedlings of 'Late Purple' sprouting broccoli, savoy cabbages and cauliflowers intended for spring harvesting.

☐ Plant out leeks. Soak the soil first and make planting holes 15cm (6in.) deep with a dibber. Drop the seedlings in 23cm (9in.) apart in rows 38cm (15in.) apart and water in.

☐ Gently spray flowers of French beans, runner beans and outdoor tomatoes with the hose in dry weather in the morning or evening to facilitate setting.

☐ Liquid-feed newly planted out celery, cabbage, sprouts, celeriac and salad crops every 10 days or so.

☐ Water outdoor cucumbers, marrows, and courgettes copiously. Apply a derris or pyrethrum insecticide to control insect pests on vegetables near to harvest. In hot weather, nicotine will give a quick knock-down of insects, and loses its toxicity in less than a day.

THE FRUIT GARDEN

Strawberries. Propagate from healthy, selected plants only. Train runners, not more than 4 per parent plant, to root in 7.5-cm (3-in.) pots, filled with good compost, sunk in the soil alongside. Cut off the extension shoot of the runners beyond the

Peg down strawberry runners into individual pots

chosen plantlets. New plants will be ready for complete severance and planting out in late August.

Pick ripe strawberries each day. Collect any fruits showing distortion, hard core or grey mould infection and burn them. Clear away and burn straw or loose mulching material after harvest. Wash down black polythene if intended for re-use.

Clear beds of strawberry plants more than 3–4 years old. They are past their best, and may harbour pests and diseases. Prepare new ground for strawberries by bastard-trenching, weeding and working in rotted manure, compost, leaf-mould, or peat liberally, ready to plant up in August-September.

☐ Thin plums bearing heavy crops, both to ensure high-quality dessert fruit, and flower-bud formation for next year.

☐ Check all stone fruits (cherries, damsons, plums) and the ornamental species of the *Prunus* genus for the silvered look on foliage that indicates silver leaf disease. Cut out cleanly any infected shoots and branches and burn them.

☐ Bury the tips of the new shoots of blackberry, boysenberry and loganberry bushes in the soil if extra plants are needed. Sever them next March if rooted, and transplant the new plants.

☐ Pinch out the growing points of the shoots on outdoor figs.

☐ Commence the summer pruning of apples and pears in late July, as new growth matures and hardens, spreading the work over a few weeks. Shorten the new growth on lateral or side shoots to within 3 leaves of their base, plus the basal rosette of leaves. Any sub-laterals are cut back to just above one leaf. Leave extension shoots of the main stem and leading branches untouched. Summer pruning aims to admit more light and air to the ripening fruits, as well as encouraging shoot growth and the development of fruit buds.

THE ORNAMENTAL GARDEN

Hedges

Trim quick-growing hedges such as thorn, *Lonicera nitida*, privet and gorse as soon as new growth begins to look spiky.

Trim informal flowering hedges of *Buddleia alternifolia*, *Ceanothus dentatus*, *Chaenomeles speciosa*, *Philadelphus* species, *Rosa moyesii*, and *Spiraea arguta* as the flowers fade, cutting the flowered shoots to within 10–15cm (4–6in.) of their base.

Clip established formal hedges of beech, box, *Euonymus japonicus*, cypress (*Chamaecyparis* and *Cupressus* species), holly, hornbeam, thuja and yew this month, after a rainy spell if possible.

☐ Prune hedges of the large-leaved evergreens – spotted laurel (*Aucuba japonica*), *Elaeagnus pungens*, cherry laurel (*Prunus laurocerasus*) and Portugal laurel (*P. lusitanica*) – with secateurs (not shears, which cut the leaves), cutting the shoots back fairly hard to just above well-placed buds or leaves.

☐ Increase plants of *Lonicera nitida* 'Ernest Wilson' and 'Fertilis' (often preferred for its stiffer, more erect growth habit) from cuttings of firm half-ripened shoots, about 23cm (9in.) long. Insert 12cm (4½in.) deep in porous soil in July or August.

☐ Propagate shrubs for low hedges of artemisia, lavender and santolina from cuttings of young new shoots, detached with a slight heel of older wood, and firmly inserted for about a third their length in porous soil.

☐ Water and overhead-spray newly planted hedges, especially Cut less closely in dry weather, and vary the direction regularly.

☐ Clear hedges of unwanted brambles, briars, bindweed and ivy. Cut the invasive plant to within 30–45cm (12–18in.) of its base. Bend over the stems or shoots into a litre bottle filled with a brushwood or glyphosate weedkiller solution. Leave for a week or two to soak up the fluid.

Lawns

☐ Treat patches of clover with a mecoprop herbicide, but related yellow-flowering plants such as hop trefoil and bird's foot trefoil need stronger treatment, such as a pinch of sulphamate of ammonia on their crowns.

☐ Regulate cutting with the now-slackening pace of growth. Cut less closely in dry weather, and vary the direction regularly.

☐ Water to soak thoroughly, when necessary, but when water restrictions are in force, spray with a liquid foliar feed to keep the grasses nurtured and growing.

☐ Prepare new lawn sites for late summer sowing. Worn out, dilapidated lawns can have the old top growth destroyed by applying a paraquat/diquat weedkiller, prior to renovation by cultivation, manuring, fertilising and re-seeding.

The Rock Garden
Plant autumn- and winter-flowering crocuses where suitable space can be found (see above, The Flower Garden).

☐ Take cuttings of spring and early-summer-flowering alpines this month and next. Select short shoots of the current year's growth, removed with a small heel of the wood of the stem from which they grow. Insert in pans, pots or boxes, filled with moist, porous compost (1 part by volume loam, 1 part peat, and 2 parts coarse sand or perlite), and place in a cold frame or greenhouse. Most hardy alpines are eligible. Heel cuttings of calluna, erica, ceratostigma, cotoneaster, and dwarf conifers can also be rooted now to give new plants.

☐ Lift plants of the tuberous-rooted *Anemone apennina*, *A. blanda* and *A. nemorosa* for division and replanting.

☐ Lift and divide the rhizomatous roots of the dwarf irises, *Iris bucharica*, *I. chamaeiris*, *I. innominata* and *I. tenax* towards the end of the month.

Roses
Dead-head bush and cluster roses, cutting clean stems to just above a leaf bud from which a new lateral shoot can develop.

Dead-head old shrub roses that flower once only and prune lightly, removing old shoots and weakly growth at the same time except in the case of those with distinctive hips forming later, such as *Rosa multibracteata*, *R.* × *highdownensis*, *R. moyesii*, *R. m.* 'Geranium', *R. pomifera* 'Duplex', *R. rubiginosa* and *R. rubrifolia*. Roses which are repeat-flowering such as bourbons, hybrid perpetuals, china, hybrid musks, rugosa and modern shrub roses, only require regular dead-heading, with pruning deferred to the winter.

☐ Propagate favourite roses – though not hybrid teas – by taking 23-cm (9-in.) cuttings of firm, maturing shoots of this year's growth, in late July. Cut below a bud, remove the leaves from the lower 15cm (6in.), insert in good soil and firm well. Cover with cloches.

Layer young shoots of climbing and rambling roses at any time from mid-July to early autumn. Bend the shoots to the ground, slitting the stems half-way through with a slanting cut from a nodal bud, 38–45cm (15–18in.) from the end. Peg or weight it down and cover it with soil. Leave to root. New plants should be ready to sever for transplanting next spring.

☐ Keep an eye open for powdery mildew in dry weather, and black spot when it turns cool and damp. A fortnightly application of a systemic fungicide controls both infections.

Aphids and other insect pests such as the rose leaf miner are best countered by the application of a systemic insecticide, or nicotine.

Shrubs

Prune May- and June-flowering shrubs as soon as flowering is over, if necessary. Cut out old worn-out stems and crowded shoots. Ceanothus, deutzia, philadelphus, and weigela may have flowered shoots shortened as much as needed. Cut back only the flowered growth on brooms, however, not into old wood.

☐ Safeguard shallow-rooting shrubs such as rhododendrons, hydrangeas, and precious magnolias in dry weather by paying particular attention to watering and mulching.

☐ Propagate shrubs that do not root readily from cuttings by layering, particularly evergreens; bending suitable low shoots to the soil, slitting halfway through or nicking behind a node at the lowest point of the bend, fastening down, and mounding over with good soil compost, to form roots. New plants should be ready for detaching next spring.

☐ Propagate shrubs from stem cuttings this month and next. Use shoots of the current year's growth, just beginning to harden or ripen. Cut cleanly below a node, where a leaf or leaves join the main stem. Remove the lower leaves on a third to a half the length of the cutting without damaging the buds or bark of the shoots. Insert the leafless part in a cuttings compost, sand or perlite. Keep it moist and shaded from hot sun.

Dipping the ends of cuttings in a root-inducing hormone solution or powder quickens initial root formation. Cuttings of some shrubs root or 'strike' easily in porous soil out of doors, under cloches. Others do better in propagating frames, with a little bottom heat. Easy subjects are abutilon, actinidia, berberis, buddleia, ceanothus, forsythia, fuchsia, hypericum, potentilla, santolina, senecio and skimmia.

Trees

Prune deciduous trees that obviously need thinning or improving in shapeliness by cutting out badly placed or overgrown branches. Cut at a junction or base, flush with the older growth, and paint cuts with a tree antiseptic or fungicidal solution. Thinning out the branches of overhanging trees admits more light to the advantage of plants growing underneath as well as the tree itself and now is the time to do it.

The Water Garden

Feed fish regularly in the summer months, preferably early in the morning and again in the afternoon. They like caterpillars, earthworms, and woodlice as well as proprietary balanced foods.

Propagate underwater oxygenating plants by detaching slips or pieces and inserting them in the bottom soil of the pool.

Hose aphids and other insects off the leaves of water lilies for the fish to dispose of.

Top up with tepid clean water to compensate for evaporation. Check the water temperature of small shallow pools on hot days, if it contains fish or plants likely to suffer in high temperatures. Shade at least part of the pool in a heat wave by a screen or tent of hessian or opaque plastic sheeting.

THE GARDEN UNDER GLASS

Take the opportunity offered by hot sunny days to clean empty frames and repaint wooden ones. Replace glass in broken cloches; clean off soil splashes and any greening by washing with a dilute fungicidal solution, prior to re-use in late summer and autumn.

☐ Treat the cool and cold greenhouse in much the same way this month. Ventilate freely when temperatures are rising. Damp down paths and surfaces daily in hot weather; mist-spray or syringe plants in the forenoon. Try to keep day temperatures equable within the range 24–27°C (75–80°F), and at night between 15.5–18°C (60–65°F). Screen open doors and ventilators with fine mesh nylon or terylene scrim to exclude insects, especially when fruit crops are ripening.

☐ Sow seeds of *Nicotiana × sanderae* and *N. suaveolens*, treating them as half-hardy annuals, to provide a sweet fragrance in November in the cool greenhouse or indoors. There is still time to sow seeds of calceolaria for a winter show.

Make a sowing of winter-flowering 'Beauty of Nice' stocks to flower in the cold or cool greenhouse in winter.

☐ Take basal cuttings of mid-season and late varieties of chrysanthemums, rooting them in peat-wood fibre pots and growing on in a cool greenhouse to flower in winter.

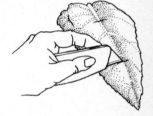

☐ Take leaf cuttings of *Begonia rex* and other begonias grown for their colourful foliage. Cut the veins or ribs at junctions with a razor blade. Lay the leaf flat, pegged down on moist compost in a seed box or pan. Cover the box and keep at 18–21°C

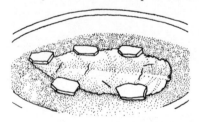
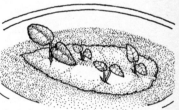

Taking leaf cuttings of *Begonia rex*

(65–70°F). Buds and young plantlets will form at the cuts; when well-rooted pot the young plants up individually.

☐ Pinch out the tops of stems of tomato plants when they have formed the sixth or seventh flower truss if you intend to bring chrysanthemums into the greenhouse for late flowering in September. Continue feeding until the end of August, and remove axillary side shoots regularly.

P.T.O.

<u>Helianthemum</u> - Dead head regularly. *Pruning is impt.-
Cut back all straggly stems once flowering over.

<u>Oxalis</u> - label the site to avoid hoeing it up in
winter, as it disappears underground.

<u>Thyme</u> - remove dead blooms with shears when flowering
finished.

August

Some August plants in flower and vegetables in season

See the June and July lists for the many plants in flower from June to August. The following appear this month:

The Flower Garden
Aster
Chrysanthemum
Clarkia
Convolvulus
Coreopsis
Echium
Erigeron
Encomis
Gentian
Hosta
Michaelmas daisy (*Aster novi-belgii*)
Montbretia
Nerine
Nigella (love-in-a-mist)
Oenothera (evening primrose)
Romneya
Saponeria
Sidalcea
Solidago (golden rod)
Tahecetum
Thyme

The Ornamental Garden
Caryopteris
Ceanothos
Clerodendron
Clematis orientalis, (*C. × viticella* varieties)
Clematis tangutica

Vegetables in season
(see July list)
Sweet corn
Onion

Fruit in season
(see July list)
Cherry
Loganberry
Pear
Plum

Although it is traditionally the holiday month, August seldom epitomises the summer. It tends to be wetter than June, July and September, its fine hot sunny spells put to an end by thunderstorms and drenching, chilling rains. It is a month of change both for plants and gardeners.

THE FLOWER GARDEN

Cut off spent flower-heads of dahlias regularly to induce further bloom. Give a liquid feed every 10 days or so.

Cut out the spent flowered stems of border plants such as delphiniums and of gladioli before they form seeds.

Disbud early chrysanthemums to give larger blooms, rubbing off the smaller side buds around the one chosen to flower. For effective sprays of bloom, on the other hand, remove the central terminal bud.

Give a liquid feed to late-flowering border plants such as Michaelmas daisies, golden rod, heleniums, and border chrysanthemums. Keep a watch for mildew in fine weather, when nights are cool and dewy, and apply a benomyl, dinocap or sulphur fungicide to control it.

☐ Prepare sites for new shrubs and trees to be planted in the autumn. If they are thick with grass and weeds, dress with a glyphosate herbicide early in the month and cultivate in 5 weeks' time safely free of weeds.

☐ Finalise your plans for autumn bulb planting, and order bulbs as soon as available. Narcissi should be planted in October, crocuses in September, but tulips can be left until November.

Finish planting of autumn-flowering bulbs and corms as soon as possible.

☐ Continue to take cuttings of herbaceous plants such as dimorphotheca, gazania, helianthemum, and pelargoniums, choosing firm, half-ripened, sturdy shoots, clean-cut below a leaf junction or node, or removed with a sliver of bark or heel of the stem, for rooting in compost containing sand or perlite. Remove the lower leaves, dip the ends in a root-inducing hormone compound (optional); and insert in pots, boxes or frames. Shade from hot sun, keep the compost moist, and transplant those which have formed roots and are showing signs of top growth.

☐ Begin lifting and potting up half-hardy plants such as begonias, hippeastrum and arum lilies to winter under cover.

THE VEGETABLE GARDEN

Prepare onions for harvesting; thrust a fork under the bulbs, lift slightly to break the roots, and bend over the tops at the neck. Harvest in 2–3 weeks on a fine day. Brush them free of soil and dry off thoroughly in a dry shed. Plait them in ropes if you like, but they will keep perfectly well in net bags or boxes in an attic or dry frost-free place.

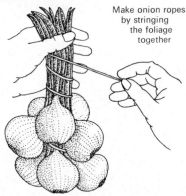

Make onion ropes by stringing the foliage together

☐ Lift second-early potatoes as soon as the haulms begin to yellow. Do not leave any longer to attract slugs or wire worms. Choose a fine day, when tubers can air-dry quickly and be freed of soil. Store in fibre-board or wooden boxes in cool, frostproof, completely dark sheds, cellars or rooms. Light reaching the tubers turns them green and poisonous.

☐ Remove the tops of outdoor tomatoes as soon as the fourth truss of flowers has formed. Liquid feed weekly, and spray with a copper fungicide if brownish-purple blotches of blight appear in the leaves.

☐ Cut the stems of broad beans and peas for composting as soon as cropping ends. Leave the roots to rot and enrich the soil with nitrogen.

☐ Finish planting out of winter brassica crops (Brussels sprouts, cabbage, sprouting broccoli and kale) early in the month, especially in the north.

Sow spring cabbage ('Flower of Spring', 'April Monarch') early in the month in a prepared seed-bed, and transplant at the end of the month.

Sow Japanese onions ('Early Kaizuka', 'Senshyu Yellow', 'Express Yellow F_1') in mid-August to crop next June–July.

☐ Examine all brassica crops on the undersides of their leaves for yellow patches of eggs or caterpillars when you see the white winged cabbage butterflies flitting about the garden. Hand-pick to destroy, or dust, or spray with a derris or pyrethrum insecticide.

☐ Gather herbs for drying, preferably in the late afternoon of a dry day. Tie by the stems in small bunches, and hang them upside down in a dry airy place; or spread out on clean paper on baking trays or in an airing cupboard. When the leaves are brittle and easily crumbled, rub them through the fingers, discard the chaff, pack into airtight containers and store in a cool place. Do not use glass jars as the herbs will lose their flavour if exposed to light.

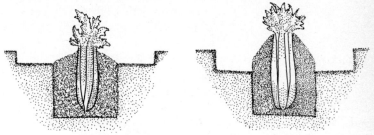

Continue to earth up celery as the stems lengthen

☐ Earth up celery after rain or watering, taking care that no soil lodges between the leaf stalks; or wrap cardboard or newspaper collars round them, to exclude light and blanch the stems. Self-blanching strains do not need this treatment.

THE FRUIT GARDEN

Strawberries. Clean up the strawberry bed after harvest. Remove all weeds, excess runners, old, yellowing or discoloured leaves, and lightly fork over the soil between the rows.

Move rooted runners intended for the new strawberry bed as soon as it is obvious they are growing strongly. Lift with soil, and space about 38cm (15in.) apart in rows 75cm (2ft 6in.)

135

apart, watering in on well-prepared ground (see July notes).

Give a dilute liquid feed to late-fruiting strawberries of the alpine types: 'Alexandria', 'Baron Solemacher', 'Fraise des Bois', or 'Red Alpine', and keep watered in dry weather.

☐ Cut away the fruited canes of raspberries at ground level and burn them so that they cannot harbour pests such as the larvae of the raspberry beetle or moth, or fungus infection. Remove weeds by hand: use of a weedkiller may destroy new canes. Pull up sucker canes growing away from the stools or retained plants.

☐ Prune the fruited canes of loganberries at soil level as soon as the crop has been harvested.

☐ Pick early varieties of apple, such as the culinary variety 'Emneth Early', and the dessert varieties 'Beauty of Bath', 'Laxton's Advance' and 'Laxton's Epicure'. Harvest with care as they bruise easily. Apples are ready to gather when they part easily from the spur on being gently lifted in the hand; no force should be necessary.

☐ Pick outdoor nectarines and peaches if ready. Cradle the fruit in the palm of the hand, and if the pulp around the stalk-end feels soft, and the fruit parts easily when gently moved to and fro, pick it. Then cut away the shoots that bore them.

☐ Prune black currants after harvest, cutting out entirely some of the older fruited shoots.

☐ Trace wasps back to their nests by watching their line of flight. At dusk place a small spoonful of pyrethrum or pirimiphos-methyl or carbaryl insecticidal dust just inside the entrance.

THE ORNAMENTAL GARDEN

Hedges
Give established hedges of beech, box, holly, thorn and yew a final clipping to reduce straggly growth and make them compact.

☐ Keep hedge bottoms clear of debris, grass and weeds – often beloved by insects, including pests, for winter shelter. Then dress with a granular weedkiller to keep weed-free.

Lawns

Prepare new lawn sites for sowing in late August (in the north) or September in the south. Make sure of good drainage. Lighten heavy sub-soils with horticultural gypsum and limestone grit. Treat a heavy top-soil with a calcareous seaweed soil conditioner. If you want to raise the level of a lawn on low-lying ground, place a 7.5–15-cm (3–6-in.) layer of crushed clinker and ash under the top 10cm (4in.) of soil. If drainage is good, however, a sunken lawn can be an attractive feature.

☐ Consolidate the disturbed soil by walking over it on your heels, in short steps. Rake and rake again to make it level. Add fine lawn peat or sifted rooted organic matter to light soils and soils short of humus, and scarify this in. Apply a balanced lawn fertiliser at half the full rate a week or two before sowing.

☐ Rake the surface to a fine crumbly finish; mark off the area in 2-m (6-ft) squares. Sow each square with 185g (6oz) of a grass seed mixture suited to the purpose of the lawn and the soil. Have the seed dressed to repel birds. Cover lightly by gentle raking. With quick germination (10–21 days) in a warm soil, grasses establish well from August sowings.

☐ Stop 'fairy rings' advancing. Circular or semi-circular arcs of various fungi – puff balls, toadstools, chanterelles or mushrooms – with outer rims of deeper green grass, and inner areas of weedy felted browning turf, call for thorough aeration by hollow-tine forking, and then the application of a benomyl systemic or a mecurised fungicide to soak the soil beneath.

The Rock Garden

Increase evergreen alpines by lifting and carefully dividing them, each part furnished with a top growth and roots. Replant immediately, watering in. Species of acaena, achillea, aster, globularia, ranunculus, sedum, sempervivum and thyme are typical eligible subjects, as is *Saxifraga oppositifolia*.

☐ Plant up with dwarf bulbs and corms such as crocus species, dwarf daffodils (*Narcissus bulbocodium, N. cyclamineus, N. triandrus*, dog's-tooth violets (*Erythronium dens-canis*), grape hyacinths (*Muscari* species), *Puschkinia scilloides, Scilla* species, *Sternbergia lutea* and winter aconites (*Eranthis hyemalis*), in pockets of well-drained soil, enriched with leaf mould, where they can remain undisturbed until crowded.

137

☐ Keep weeds, especially perennials, from becoming entrenched. Remove them by hand if possible or spot-treat with a total weedkiller by brush or injection.

Roses

Continue to watch for blackspot infection in damp weather. Collect and burn fallen and badly blotched leaves, and then applying a systemic fungicide or one based on captan.

Treat new leaves reduced to a skeleton of veins by the caterpillars of the yellow-tail or buff-tip moth with a derris or malathion insecticide.

☐ Switch from a high-nitrogen to a high-phosphorus fertiliser if feeding late in the season to avoid soft shoot growth. Plants need phosphorus and potash rather than nitrogen to ripen new wood.

Pruning. Wichuraiana rambler roses, such as 'Crimson Shower', 'Dorothy Perkins', 'Excelsa' and 'Sanders' White', can be pruned now by taking the flowered shoots right out at the base and training in the new growth to flower next year.

Prune the large-flowering Wichuraiana ramblers, such as 'Albertine', 'Albéric Barbier', 'Chaplin's Pink Climber', 'Easlea's Golden Rambler', 'Emily Gray', 'Leontine Gervais', 'Paul's Scarlet Climber' and 'Thelma', less severely, simply removing one or more of the older stems occasionally at ground level and training in replacement shoots, shortening lateral shoots to about 8 to 9 buds or leaves.

Do as little as possible to the repeat-flowering climbers such as 'Autumn Sunlight', 'Casino', 'Compassion', 'Danse du Feu', 'Golden Showers', 'Handel', 'New Dawn' and 'Swan Lake', merely removing weak and badly placed shoots and cutting out a little older wood only.

Shrubs

Take heeled cuttings of plants you wish to increase throughout the month. Select sturdy, healthy, lateral and non-flowered shoots, semi-ripe or just beginning to harden, detached with bases or heels of wood from the parent stem, which contain a concentration of growth cells ready to bud roots freely. Among the many species propagated in this way are berberis, cotoneaster, deutzia, escallonia, forsythia, fothergilla, fuchsia, garrya, honeysuckle, hydrangea, hypericum, jasmine, lavender, philadelphus, potentilla, rhododendron, stuartia, syringa, vaccinium and viburnum. Dip the ends of the cuttings in hormone rooting powder and insert in pots of equal parts by volume peat and sand. Keep in a cold frame or better still a propagating unit with bottom heat of 13–16°C (55–61°F) until the cuttings have rooted. Pot on into John Innes potting compost No. 2 and overwinter in a cold frame.

☐ Prepare badly placed shrubs or small trees for moving. Dig a trench around the plant, corresponding to the reach of the branches, to 45cm (18in.) deep. Undercut by thrusting a sharp spade down and under the top roots to sever them. Fill in the trench with moist peat or pulverised bark, until it is time to make the removal in autumn or next spring, when the plant can be lifted with its roots intact in a soil ball. It is unwise to attempt to move very large, older specimens. They stand little chance of adjusting to root-pruning.

Trees
Stop regrowth from the stumps of felled trees by spraying all exposed surfaces with a brushwood killer. Have large stumps cleared professionally by tree surgeons. Small stumps can usually be removed piecemeal, splitting them with steel timber wedges and cutting the main roots with axe and saw. Quick chemical destruction is seldom possible, nor is it economical.

The Water Garden
Have a frame or cover of fine-mesh plastic netting on hand to place over small pools for shade on very hot days and to break the force of chilling downpours when thunderstorms break.

☐ Reduce spreading duckweed by hosing it to one corner or side of the pool, and removing it with a scoop. It is not injurious to fish or pool life, but can multiply quickly and obscure everything. Remove it this month before hibernating buds are formed and sink to the bottom of the pool.

☐ If the fish are gulping at the surface play a fine spray of water over the pool in very hot weather. This helps to step up the oxygen level of the water. Let the spray fall through the air from as high as possible. As well as being decorative, a fountain is the permanent remedy for this problem, but precludes the cultivation of, for example, water lilies.

THE GARDEN UNDER GLASS

Use empty space in frames for the propagation of perennial plants and shrubs from softwood or half-ripe cuttings.

☐ Move frost-vulnerable half-hardy perennials such as pelargoniums and tuberous begonias to frames or the greenhouse towards the end of the month in the north.

☐ Repot tubers of *Cyclamen persicum* varieties now beginning to make new growth, with the tops of tubers at surface level. Pot on young plants, raised from seeds, for winter flowering.

Lift roots of the arum or calla lily (*Zantedeschia aethiopica*) and plant up in large pots to grow cool under glass for spring

☐ Take cuttings of promising greenhouse shrubs and perennials – half-ripened, non-flowered shoots, either cut beneath a node or taken with a 'heel' of basal older bark – to root in a propagating unit at about 18°C (65°F). Let soft cuttings such as those of pelargoniums lie on the staging overnight for cut surfaces to dry and callous.

Take stem cutting with a heel (left) or basal shoot (right)

☐ Pot specially prepared bulbs of hyacinths for Christmas flowering; Roman hyacinths for late November–December flowering; and polyanthus narcissi ('Paper White', 'Soleil d'Or') for Christmas and new year flowering, about the middle of the month, in bulb fibre or compost. Place the pots at the base of a north-facing wall or fence, covered with ashes, leaves or wood chippings and sawdust. Leave them for 6 or 7 weeks or until shoots are about 2.5cm (1in.) above compost level before bringing into the cool greenhouse for forcing and flowering. Bulbs for forcing need a cool, dark period while roots are formed.

☐ Pot up bulbs of *Lachenalia bulbifera* and hybrids early in the month for Christmas and new year flowering. *L. aloides* and its varieties flower a little later. Use John Innes No. 2 compost. Keep at 10–13°C (50–55°F).

☐ Withhold water from gloxinias (*Sinningia speciosa*) now finishing flowering. Dry the tubers off and rest them under cool conditions, not less than 10°C (50°F).

☐ Feed chrysanthemums as they come into bud, every 7 to 10 days, with a balanced proprietary chrysanthemum fertiliser or nitrate of potash solution (15g/4.5 litres of water) ($\frac{1}{2}$oz per gallon).

☐ Feed tomatoes regularly, especially if in soil-less compost, rings or grow-bags, with a balanced fertiliser high in potash. Trickle-watering does much to avoid troubles such as blossom end rot, dry set, and failure of fruits to swell normally. Add a pinch of Epsom salts (magnesium sulphate) to the water to prevent yellowing and withering of lower leaves.

☐ Remove lower leaves as fruiting trusses are harvested. Take heed of these symptoms: yellow-green mosaic mottling of leaves, brown spots and brown streaks on stems, stunted bushy growth, twisted, tendril-like leaves and bronzing and downward curling of leaves. If such symptoms persist and affect the whole plant, it is probably virus disease. There is no cure, only prevention of its spread by removing infected plants and burning them.

☐ Yellowing blotches above and below tomato leaf surfaces, particularly in coolish, muggy weather, could indicate leaf mould. If a brownish-purple mould develops, remove badly infected leaves and spray with a sulphur fungicide. Next year grow a leaf mould-resistant variety.

☐ Harvest cucumbers as soon as the fruits have grown plump and full. Keep well watered but avoid wet conditions around the base of plants, which are susceptible to canker or foot rot. Pale areas on the leaves, which turn dry and brown, indicate the fungus disease anthracnose. Destroy affected leaves and apply a sulphur fungicide. Yellow mottling or mosaic, however, may be a virus infection, for which there is no cure.

141

P. T. O.

(SMELLY YELLOW)

Alchemilla – once flowering has finished, cut plant back to just above ground level.

Honeysuckle – remove unwanted stems when flowering is over. Remove some of the old stems.

Lavender – Remove stalks when flowers fade.

September

Some September plants in flower and vegetables in season

See July and August lists for plants continuing to flower.
The following appear this month:

The Flower Garden
Anemone hupehensis, A. japonica
Cimicifuga
Colchicum (autumn crocus)
Cyclamen neapolitum
Gladiolus
Viola
Zauschneria

Grasses
Cortaderia selloana
Cyperus longus
Miscanthus

Trees and Shrubs with colourful fruits
Berberis
Chaenomeles (flowering quince, japonica)
Cotoneaster
Euonymus (spindle)
Hawthorn
Maple
Pyracantha
Sorbus (mountain ash)
Viburnum

Vegetables in season
(see July and August lists)
Cabbage
Cauliflower
Celery
Spinach beet
Tomato

Fruit in season
Apple
Apricot
Blackberry
Damson
Peach
Pear
Plum

September weather, no less than that of any other month in Britain, can be changeable, but on the whole it is drier than August, and mild spells permit a good harvest. Latitude, proximity to the sea, and altitude combine, however, to affect the duration of sunlight received each day, and must increasingly be taken into account in timing gardening operations. The further north, the further inland and the higher a garden, the earlier autumn and winter are likely to visit it, and pre-winter tasks, usually need to be advanced by 1 to 3 weeks.

THE FLOWER GARDEN

Dead-head border flowers as they fade, and cut back stems while green to make compost.

Divide spring and early summer-flowering border plants if overcrowded. Discard the older central parts and replant the younger ones immediately.

☐ Start bulb and corm planting this month, particularly the smaller bulbs of chionodoxa, fritillaria, irises, muscari, *Narcissus* species, ornithogalum puschkinia and scilla. Broadly, the earlier they are expected to flower, the earlier they should be put to bed. Plant the corms of crocus and the tubers and rhizomes of *Anemone* species, eranthis, erythronium and ranunculus as soon as possible, especially in the north. They dry out quickly when left in the air. Hyacinths, large daffodil and narcissus bulbs and tulips can wait until October–November, if necessary, but lose nothing by being planted earlier. Place at a depth equal to twice their own width in the soil. Set on a layer of sand in clay soils.

☐ Plant the flowering onions (*Allium* species) this month and next, in sunny positions and humus-enriched soil.

Give the large bulbs of crown imperials (*Fritillaria imperialis*) a sunny south aspect, in a deeply worked and rich soil. Set them on their sides, to prevent moisture collecting in the dimple, 15cm (6in.) deep.

☐ Plant out herbaceous perennials, and pinks raised from cuttings earlier in the year, where they are to flower.

Begin planting out biennials to their final flowering positions in the latter half of the month.

Make sowings of hardy annuals such as calendula, cornflower, eschscholzia, gypsophilia, larkspur, mallow, scabious, love-in-a-mist, Shirley poppy and pansies on open sites to provide early colourful spring bloom next year.

THE VEGETABLE GARDEN

Continue to lift potatoes this month and next when the haulms start to yellow, as there will be no further growth in the tubers (see August notes).

Lift mature root crops towards the end of the month. Remove tops close to the crowns, and store beetroot and carrots layered in sand in boxes or bins, placed in a cool cellar or shed. Safeguard from mice and rats by enclosing in fine-mesh netting, or put down a suitable bait. Carrots can also be stored in an outdoor clamp. Parsnips, salsify and scorzonera can be left in the ground until needed.

Earth up celery and leeks being grown in trenches. Stake plants of Brussels sprouts and sprouting broccoli exposed to wind.

☐ Harvest all the tomatoes from outdoor plants at the first hint of frost, or when night temperatures drop below 10°C (50°F). Simply place green fruits in paper bags in a warm room to ripen; since warmth, not light, ripens them, it is a waste of time putting them in rows on the windowsills.

THE FRUIT GARDEN

☐ Gather plums for cooking as soon as they begin to show colour. For dessert purposes, however, leave them on the trees until fully ripe. Remove the fruits with stalks attached, but do not attempt to keep beyond a week or so. Gather blue-black sweet damsons from mid-September onwards.

☐ Plant up the new strawberry bed as soon as possible. The ground should be free of perennial weeds and their roots, and liberally enriched with rotted manure, good compost, horticultural peat or composted forestry bark, and organic fertilisers, not chemicals. Soak plants before setting them in with their crowns at ground level. Water

Plant strawberry crowns level with the soil surface and spread out the roots

daily in dry weather until they are obviously established. Make
sure that plants purchased are certified to be virus-free stock.

Set out maiden plants of the so-called 'perpetual' fruiting
varieties, 30cm (12in.) apart in rows, to give strawberries from
July to October. Crops are obtained for one, at the most two,
years with vigorous varieties such as 'Gento'. These can be used
as front-of-border or edging plants.

☐ Harvest the early cooking and dessert apples as they ripen,
that is, when the fruits part readily from the spur when lifted
and given a slight twist. Fruits that have to be tugged or pulled
off are not ripe enough. Leave late-keeping varieties until late
September or October, and go over the trees several times.

Gather pears just before they are ripe, as soon as the stalk
parts from the spur when the fruit is lifted to the near vertical.
If left too long they turn mealy and lose their sweetness.

☐ Put greasebands around the trunks of standard apples and
pears just below the first branch junction, and on the main
branches of bush trees near their base, to trap insects such as
wingless winter moths, March moths, codling moths and capsid
bugs seeking to lay their eggs in bark crevices. Inspect from
time to time and remove and replace as necessary.

☐ Harvest cob and filbert nuts fully ripe for storage. Wait until
the husks are brown and the nuts are freed easily.

☐ Cut out the fruited canes of blackberries and other hybrid
bramble berries at ground level after harvest and train in the
new developing shoots to take their place.

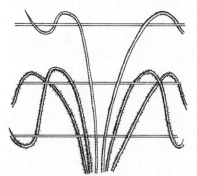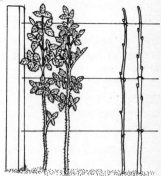

Training systems for blackberries (left) and raspberries (right) keep new and fruiting wood
separate and make picking and pruning easier

THE ORNAMENTAL GARDEN

Hedges

Give a final clipping to quick-growing hedges being grown to formal shapes.

☐ Take cuttings of the cherry laurel (*Prunus laurocerasus*) early in the month. Young lateral 'heeled' shoots root freely in warm moist soil. Detach heeled shoots of hedging conifers for propagation early in the month to root in porous soil in a frame or sheltered spot.

Propagate privet (*Ligustrum ovalifolium*, *L. o.* 'Aureum') from heeled shoots, 15–20cm (6–8in.) long, inserted for half their length in a V-shaped trench made with the spade, and filled with moist sand.

Paths

Cut out bare, worn turf on grass paths with a half-moon and spade. Fork over the soil and dress it with a little superphosphate. Lay replacement turf and sprinkle with grit or coarse sand. Grass paths in danger of being worn out from constant use may be better replaced by stone or concrete flags, let in to soil level.

Lawns

(See also October notes.) Sow new lawns as soon as the site is ready, preferably before mid-September in the north. Seeds germinate more readily in warm soil, and seedling plants can get well established before winter (see August notes).

☐ Repair and renovate worn patches in recreation lawns as soon as they are free. Take up the old worn turf, fork over the soil, dress with an autumn lawn fertiliser, firm and re-turf with new pieces.

The Rock Garden

Plant dwarf bulbs and corms for early spring flowering in groups (see above, The Flower Garden.)

☐ Plant hardy alpines out of pots to fill empty spaces, and ring with a 'mulch' of small chippings or gravel to aid drainage and keep the crowns dry. This is the best time of the year to establish new plants.

Roses
Take more cuttings of well-ripened shoots of the present year's growth (see August notes). White, cream, pink, and red self-coloured varieties root most easily, and old roses such as 'Gloire de Dijon', but do not expect flowers for at least two years.

☐ Keep the rose-bed clear of fallen leaves. Stop supplementary feeding so that plants can form firm, sturdy wood before the winter.

Shrubs
Propagate evergreen shrubs by layering this month. *Arbutus unedo*, aucuba, box, eucryphia, hamamelis, holly, magnolia, osmanthus and rhododendron are some of the types that can be increased in this way. Choose a low-growing shoot that can be bent down to the ground with about 15cm (6in.) of the growing point above ground. Make a small nick in the bark on the underside of the shoot at the lowest point, open up the cut and fasten it down with a wooden peg or piece of wire, and mound over with soil. Leave for one or two years, until the new plant is rooting freely. Sever it on the side nearest the parent plant, lift carefully and plant out with roots in a soil ball.

☐ Plant evergreen shrubs from mid-September, the earlier the better as far as their future welfare is concerned. This is a good time to plant winter-flowering specimens – *Erica herbacea*, *E. × darleyensis*, *E. erigena* and their varieties; forms of *Hamamelis mollis*, *H. japonica*; *Jasminum nudiflorum Mahonia japonica* and *Lonicera purpusii*.

Trees
Begin planting evergreen and coniferous trees towards the end of the month. Prepare planting stations by breaking up the second spit and enriching the top spit with moist peat or pulverised bark. If the ground is not ready, planting can wait until October or early November, but earlier planting is better as the trees can get established while the soil is still warm.

The Water Garden
Remove weeds such as docks, willow-herb, grasses and unwanted reeds. Thin out aquatic plants which have made over-vigorous growth.

☐ Divide bog and marginal aquatic plants for increase. Lift, split and replant the younger portions of plants such as *Acorus calamus*, *Butomus umbellatus*, marsh marigold (*Caltha palustris*), *Cyperus* species, *Juncus effusus*, *Pontederia cordata*, arrowhead (*Sagittaria japonica*), bulrush (*Scirpus* species), reed mace (*Typha* species), *Astilbe* species, day lily (*Hemerocallis* species), *Hosta*, *Mimulus* and *Trollius* species, before they begin their winter rest.

Remove decaying leaves from water lilies and other pool plants before they can sink to the bottom of the pool and rot. Stretch a 20-mm (¾-in.) mesh plastic net over the pool for the autumn to catch falling leaves which might otherwise foul the water in winter.

Start to reduce the food ration of fish as the temperature drops at the end of the month. Do it gradually, giving no more than what the fish will immediately consume and giving less as their movements become more sluggish.

THE GARDEN UNDER GLASS

Make a sowing of early maturing carrots ('Amsterdam Forcing', 'Early Market Horn', 'Konfrix') in frames or under cloches early in the month. Sow a hardy lettuce ('Winter Density') this month and next to winter under cloches and head up in spring. Also a quick-maturing radish ('Saxerre', 'Cherry Belle', or 'Scarlet Globe') and salad onions can now be grown.

Have cloches on hand to cover frost-tender plants.

The Cool Greenhouse
Keep temperatures in the greenhouse as equable as possible; ventilate freely if daytime temperature rises to avoid the clammy atmosphere that encourages fungus disease. Close up early before the cool of night. Stop damping down on cool cloudy days.

☐ Carry on potting up bulbs, hyacinths, narcissi and tulips, each week or fortnight, so that a number can be forced to give a succession of blooms for the new year and winter months. Place bulbs in a dark, cool place, not an airing cupboard, for 6 weeks or so until at least 5cm (2in.) of shoot shows through. At this point move them into subdued and then better light over a few days. Alternatively, place them outdoors under a north wall (see August notes). *Iris tingitana* may also be treated in this way.

Pot up freesia corms, about 6 to a 15-cm (6-in.) pot filled with John Innes No. 2 compost, and place them in the dark with other bulbs. After 6 weeks bring them into the light and do not let the temperature fall below 15.5°C (60°F) by day, 10°C (50°F) at night.

☐ Grow *Cyclamen persicum* and its varieties on under cool conditions (maximum temperature 15.5°C (60°F)). Water without wetting the top of the corms, and give a liquid feed every 10 days from when the buds show to flowering.

Bring in chrysanthemums which have been growing in pots out of doors towards the end of the month. Clean up the pots, remove flagging leaves and water very moderately until the plants adjust to their new conditions.

Remove tomato plants to make room for the chrysanthemums and other winter-flowering subjects. Chimney bellflower (*Campanula pyramidalis*) makes a beautiful plant, in a large pot, for early winter.

☐ Wipe down glass and greenhouse structure that is greening with algae with a cleaning solution.

Line the greenhouse with an anti-condensation plastic sheeting, fastened with clips or tape, as a kind of double-glazing that will conserve heat and increase the possibilities for growing plants in winter.

Overhaul and repair heating units for the cool greenhouse. Have electrical equipment and propagators tested. Clean oil heaters thoroughly, wipe dry the exterior parts and renew the wicks.

Make use of fine days to repair and repaint greenhouse structures; seal in glass with fresh putty where necessary, or make windproof with sealing glazing tape.

Lavender - remove stalks when flowers fade.

October

Some October plants in flower and vegetables in season

The Flower Garden
Aconitum
Anemone hupehensis
Aster
Astilbe
Cimicifuga
Chrysanthemum
Helenium
Michaelmas daisy (*Aster novi belgii*)
Penstemon
Red hot poker
Schizostylis
Solidago (golden rod)
Sunflower

Grasses
Cortaderia selloana
Miscanthus
Panicum

Trees and Shrubs with colourful fruits
Amelanchier
Arbutus
Berberis
Chaenomeles (flowering quince, japonica)
Cotoneaster
Hawthorn
Maple
Pyracantha
Skimmia japonica
Rosa rubrifolia
Sorbus (mountain ash)
Viburnum

Vegetables in season
Artichoke, globe
Beet, seakale
Brussels sprouts
Cabbage
Cauliflower
Celery
Parsnip
Spinach beet
Sweet corn
Tomato
Turnip

Fruit in season
Apple
Grape
Peach
Pear
Plum

The pace of change is, as ever, dictated by the weather, both general and local. Autumn comes earlier further north and on higher ground. The daily rises and falls in temperature are at lower levels and sharper. As mentioned under September, most tasks have to be carried out earlier in northern gardens. October is seldom without its warm spells and the weather may turn markedly mild in the later part of the month or early November. Take advantage of such spells: finish the harvest, lift frost-tender plants and give them winter protection, and get under way plans for soil cultivations and new plantings.

THE FLOWER GARDEN

Take up gladioli corms from mid-month without waiting for the frost to kill the top growth. With stems attached, the plants can hang in an airy place until the corms are completely dry. Retain the large top new corms, and the younger corms for increasing the stock for next year; discard the old shrunken ones. Dust with flowers of sulphur and store layered in sand or perlite, in boxes, in a cool, frostproof place. The cormlets can be stored for the winter and planted in reserve beds in spring to grow on to flowering size.

In the north lift the corms of hybrid crocosmia ('montbretia') after flowering, dry off the corms and store as gladioli.

☐ Lift dahlia roots intact with tubers as soon as the top growth is blackened by a night frost. Cut the stems to within 5cm (2in.) of their base, remove surplus soil, leave to dry upside down under cover, and when dry, store in boxes or crates. Label them and dust with a fungicidal powder before storing in a dark cool place, cellar or spare room, where there is an even temperature of about 7°C (45°F).

Take up the stools or roots of border chrysanthemums when flowering is over. Cut the stems to about 5–7.5cm (2–3in.), and place in a deep box or cold frame just as they are, with added soil to cover, where the temperature will not fall below 1.6°C (35°F).

Lift clumps of lily-of-the-valley (*Convallaria majalis* and varieties) now 3 to 4 years old. Divide and replant the strong crowns just clear of one another, and with points just at soil

155

level. The new planting stations should be deeply dug and enriched with well-rotted manure or compost, and a little bone meal, in partial shade.

☐ Remove annual bedding plants as soon as flowering is over, and while they are still green, and make compost with them. Fork a dressing of well-rotted manure, compost or spent mushroom compost, with bone meal into the flower bed, and plant up with bulbs and polyanthus, pansies or wallflowers for spring.

Cut down and remove stems and top growth of herbaceous perennials in the border; crush or chop tough material before adding to the compost heap. Remove stakes and clean them before storing.

Lift to divide long-established peonies early in the month; discard the older parts of the roots taking care not to damage the remainder and replant the other pieces, comprising good crown buds with roots, in well-dug soil enriched with humus-forming organic matter, and basic slag. Do not expect the new plants to flower for a year or two while they recover as they are susceptible to the shock of transplanting.

THE VEGETABLE GARDEN

Finish carefully lifting potatoes, beetroot and carrots, for winter storing of undamaged specimens (see September notes). Celeriac has the advantage that it can remain in the ground until December.

Cut down the tall stems of Jerusalem artichokes as soon as they flag and yellow. Leave the tubers undisturbed, however, and harvest as required. A good covering of leaves will make this possible in frosty weather.

Cut away all remaining fern or top growth of asparagus. Weed the bed and dress with 5–7.5cm (2–3in.) of farmyard manure or good compost, with a layer of soil sprinkled on top, for winter.

Cut down the stems of globe artichokes to ground level; cover the plants with a thick layer of peat, sawdust, leaves or bracken.

Give a final earthing-up to maincrop winter celery, carefully packing the soil up to the tips of the plants. This is essential to prevent bacteria entering which may cause celery heart rot.

THE FRUIT GARDEN

Apples. Continue to harvest as they ripen (see September notes). As a general guide, the longer an apple variety keeps, the later it should be picked. Store under cool, well-ventilated, dampish rather than dry conditions, at an even temperature between 5–7°C (40–45°F). Space without touching on racks or slatted shelves or, if not available, wrap choice fruit separately in oiled papers to preserve flavour. Inspect stored fruit regularly and remove any that go soft or smell rotten.

Pears. Harvest late-keeping varieties such as 'Josephine de Malines', 'Easter Beurré', 'Duchess de Bordeaux', 'Bellissime d'Hiver' and 'Catillac' when well coloured and easily parted from the tree. Place them straight in store, separately, preferably not wrapped as this tends to speed the ripening of pears. Do not store with apples.

Raspberries. Gather the fruit of autumn-bearing varieties such as 'Zeva' on dry days, but leave the canes intact until February–March, when they should be cut back to soil level. Earlier fruiting raspberries should have their fruited canes cut out now, if not already removed.

Walnuts. Harvest this month, as soon as they begin to fall. Remove the outer loose husk with a wire brush; then store the nuts in a cool place in boxes, in layers, each layer just covered with sand.

Currants. Take cuttings of black currant, consisting of this year's shoots, 20–25cm (8–10in.) long, cut below a bud. Leaving all the buds intact, insert in a trench in porous soil, with 2 buds only above ground level, and firm well. Plant out one year later, if rooted.

Take cuttings of red and white currants and gooseberries in the same way, but remove all the lower buds, leaving about 3 on the part of the shoot above ground. The resultant plants will then have a single main stem, and can be grown on as cordon plants or standards.

☐ Prune wall-trained morello cherries. Cut out old fruited shoots and barren branches, to give new shoot growth an opportunity to grow when trained and tied in to wires. Dab cut ends of branches with a tree fungicidal dressing or bitumen paint.

THE ORNAMENTAL GARDEN

Hedges

Make a final clean-up of hedge bottoms to reduce the hibernation quarters for insect pests. The cleared ground can be planted with snowdrop bulbs, or primroses, if the hedge is deciduous. Both will be happy under the shelter of the branches.

☐ Plant evergreen hedges this month and next. The classical hedges of box, holly or yew suit all soils with decent drainage and a humus content. They need a year to become well established, and then make growth of 25–30cm (10–12in.) annually. The high initial cost is offset by ease in maintenance, and longevity. Holly is the only safe choice where grazing animals have access.

Plant *Buxus sempervirens* 'Suffruticosa' for low evergreen surrounds or edges to beds in traditional style.

☐ Plant coniferous hedges and screens this month and next. Leyland's Cypress (× *Cupressocyparis leylandii*), is the fastest-growing, both for screens and hedges to be curtailed and clipped; it is hardy and tolerant of most soils and conditions. Other possibilities are *Chamaecyparis lawsoniana* in many forms; the species itself needs annual trimming, but cultivars of narrow habit and limited height make good dense screens. *Thuja plicata* is good for all but cold districts and tolerates shade and chalk soil.

For flowering evergreen hedges, consider laurustinus (*Viburnum tinus*) with white or pink flowers, or *Osmarea × burkwoodii* with white flowers.

If you choose *Berberis darwinii* (rich yellow flowers), *Escallonia* hybrids (flowers pale pink to deep rose), *Mahonia aquifolium* (deep yellow flowers), *Pyracantha crenulata* 'Rogersiana' (white flowers), or *Hebe × andersonii*, (lavender flowers, south and west coastal gardens), allow room for their flowering sprays.

Paths

Make and re-make paths before winter, especially if of concrete. Give any path subjected to heavy traffic a 10-cm (4-in.) foundation layer of broken brick, stone aggregate or clinker and ash, irrespective of the finished surface.

Eradicate grass and weeds in cracks and crannies by dressing with a total weedkiller.

Lawns

Aerate lawns that have had hard wear by spiking, slitting or hollow-tine forking, to relieve compaction and facilitate penetration of autumnal top dressings and feeds.

☐ Apply a 5 per cent solution of tar-oil was to areas becoming coated with growths of moss and lichen. There will be a browning of the grasses in a few days, but they soon recover. Aerate the turf and give it a liquid feed.

Get rid of excessive worm-casts by scattering them with the back of a spring-toothed rake as a top-dressing.

☐ Top-dress according to the soil characteristics. On clay and heavy soils, apply a mixture of equal parts by volume of coarse sand and sifted organic material such as lawn peat, or compost. For strongly acid soils, include ground limestone. On light, sandy soils, use equal parts by volume loam or topsoil and organic matter. On chalk soils, use a fine lawn grade of sphagnum moss peat. On soils subject to waterlogging, use coarse grit or sand, and mix with 20 per cent crushed charcoal. Apply up to 3mm ($\frac{1}{8}$in.) thick, and brush or 'switch' in.

Feed the grass with the top-dressing. Choose a fertiliser relatively high in phosphates, low in nitrogen, and balanced in potash at this season: a proprietary blended autumn lawn fertiliser, or a mixture of equal parts by weight bone meal and powdered seaweed manure at 60g/m² (2oz per sq. yd).

☐ Cut new lawns sown in August–September when the grass reaches 5cm (2in.) high, and reduce by half; repeat in a few weeks' time.

Weed chamomile lawns by hand or spot treatment, as selective lawn weedkillers would check, if not kill, the chamomile.

The Rock Garden

Remove leaves and dying remains of plants and carry out a final weeding before the winter – by hand or by spot-treating with a contact weedkiller.

Top-dress established alpines with a mixture of equal parts by volume of fine leaf mould and coarse sand or fine grit. Mulch alpines from high altitudes, which need perfect drainage, with stone chippings – granite or sandstone for those disliking lime, limestone for the lime-tolerant – to prevent rotting of the collar and basal crown.

☐ Provide hairy or woolly-leaved alpines with a rain-shedding cover of glass or clear plastic.

Roses
Prepare ground for new rose-beds and November planting (see November notes). Time spent now creating a favourable situation for new bushes will be repaid many times over. Healthy well-established plants not only look more attractive but are much better able to withstand attacks from pests and the threat of disease. Spread the hard work of digging and incorporating well-rotted organic matter into the second spit evenly through the month. Make sure that drainage is efficient. Improve clay soils by dressing with horticultural gypsum soil conditioner. Add lime if necessary to bring within a range of pH 6.0–6.5. There is some truth in the tradition that roses do well on clay – if drainage is adequate. The best improver of light sands and chalk soils for roses is a few loads of stiff clay, evenly distributed and forked in. Work out a design for the new rose bed before planting it up, bearing in mind accessibility of each plant for pruning, dead-heading and other essential maintenance tasks, as well as the colour scheme and general overall appearance.

☐ Move roses that need transplanting within the garden. Shorten the coarse woody roots with pruners; replant with the area of the bud union slightly below soil level, and firm well into the soil.

Shrubs
Complete planting of evergreen shrubs as soon as possible, especially in the north, so that their roots can keep the leaves nurtured during the winter. Low temperatures and frost can be fatal to newly planted shrubs if planted too late.

☐ Plant deciduous shrubs in congenial weather and when the soil is easily worked between now and next March, though the earlier they are planted, the more quickly they are likely to re-establish themselves (see November notes).

Trees

Transplant trees prepared previously with a
peat-filled trench around the ball of roots, by
re-opening the trench and undercutting the
root system, first on one side so that a rolled-
up sheet of hessian or plastic can be slipped
under; and then on the other side, when the
tree can be canted over and the sheet pulled
through to enclose the roots and enable the
plant to be lifted with the roots in a large soil
ball. Replant immediately in a prepared
location, stake, and firm soil around it well.
Water liberally.

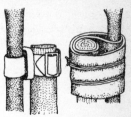

Attach newly planted
trees to stakes with a
figure-of-8 binding or
insert a buffer to prevent
chafing the bark

The Water Garden

Do not let leaves and withered plant remains sink to the bottom
of the pool, where their decomposition will lower the oxygen
content of the water for the fish.

Remove frost-sensitive floating plants such as water hyacinth
(*Eichornia crassipes*) and water lettuce (*Pistia stratiotes*) to winter
indoors in a frostproof cool greenhouse.

Remove submersible pumps for cleaning and overhaul, then
store until April–May.

Resist feeding the fish when they have become sluggish and
are inclined to stay deep in the water – even if a temporary mild
spell quickens them to cruise near the surface, as the food will
be ill-digested and upsetting.

Float a large piece of cork in small pools in case the water
should freeze over completely; or better still, install a small
electric immersion heater – to keep a small area of open water
through which toxic gases from decaying vegetation can escape,
and fresh oxygen enter the water.

☐ Plant bulbs of Quamash (*Camassia esculenta*, *C. cusickii*, *C.
leichtlinii*) in the bog garden about 7.5–10cm (3–4in.) deep.
Leave them undisturbed for 4 years, before thinning out
becomes necessary.

Plant evergreen ferns such as the hart's-tongue ferns,
Phyllitis scolopendrium and varieties, *Polypodium vulgare* and
varieties, and *Blechnum tabulare*, in moist marginal soils for
winter colour and cover. Useful deciduous species are the hardy
maidenhair, *Adiantum pedatum*; the lady fern, *Athyrium filix-*

femina, the ostrich feather fern, *Matteuccia struthiopteris*; the sensitive fern, *Onoclea sensibilis*; the royal fern, *Osmunda regalis*; and the shield fern, *Polystichum setiferum* 'Divisilobum', for waterside or streamside planting, as well as in marginal ground.

Clear poolside flags and stones of green algae growth by swabbing with a mop or cloth wrung out in a 5 per cent tar oil wash solution, without letting this get into the pool itself.

THE GARDEN UNDER GLASS

Prepare ground out of doors on which crops are to be grown under cloches early next year. Dig them over thoroughly and incorporate humus-forming organic manure or compost, and slow-release organic fertilisers, such as hoof and horn meal and bone meal, and powdered seaweed manure for potash. Do not use the same ground for cloches 2 years running without thorough cultivation and replenishment of plant food by adding balanced fertilisers.

☐ Complete the planting up of bulbs in pots or bowls for forcing in the new year (see August and September notes). Pot up a few of the less hardy uncommon corms such as *Brodiaea laxa*, *B. × tubergenii*, *Ixia viridiflora*, *Sparaxis tricolor*, *Tritonia hyalina* and *T. rosea*. Use John Innes potting compost as a growing medium and plunge the pots in moist peat in a cold frame for 6 weeks, before bringing them into the cool greenhouse to flower in spring.

Pot up plants of *Dicentra spectabilis* and *D. eximia* and place in a cold frame for 6 weeks, before bringing into the cold or cool greenhouse for gentle forcing and flowering in February.

Pot up young plants of cinerarias, raised from summer-sown seeds, into 15-cm (6-in.) pots, and bring into the cool greenhouse at about 13°C (55°F) in the latter half of the month for winter flowering.

☐ Transfer plants of *Primula malacoides*, *P. obconica* and *P. sinensis* varieties from cold frame to cool greenhouse.

Pot solomon's seal, *Polygonatum multiflorum*, and place in a cold frame for a few weeks before bringing into a cool greenhouse for forcing, and providing most attractive March–April flowers.

Give chrysanthemums free ventilation as much as possible

during the middle of the day, water in the morning, and detach yellowing leaves promptly.

☐ Pot up rose bushes in 20-cm (8-in.) pots in John Innes No. 2 compost. Stand the pots outside on ashes or boards, well-sheltered, until December; then prune the bushes and bring the pots into the greenhouse, cold or cool, watering moderately at first, then more liberally as growth is made.

Strip glass of any remaining shading material with proprietary glass cleaner or washing soda solution, and then hose down.

Peat on alchemilla (smelly yellow) - cover the crowns.

November

Some November plants in flower and vegetables in season

The Flower Garden	The Ornamental Garden	Vegetables in season
Autumn crocus	*Lonicera standishii*	Artichokes, Jerusalem
Cyclamen	Mahonia	Brussels sprouts
Gentian	*Prunus subhirtella autumnalis*	Cabbage
Iris unguicularis	Viburnum	Chicory
Nerine	Winter Jasmine	Parsnip
Schizostylis		Spinach beet
		Swede

This is the time to start soil cultivations, to replenish and increase the organic content of the soil with the humus-forming materials on which fertility is founded. November also marks the opening of the planting season, particularly for deciduous shrubs and trees and herbaceous perennials.

Soil cultivations

Start as soon as possible before the onset of winter rains and hard weather, bearing in mind that the main objectives are to break up the texture, admit air and the weathering agents, make it easier for roots to penetrate and spread, and improve both texture and nutrient level by incorporating well-rotted organic matter.

Cultivate soils heavy and dense with clay as deeply as possible; a flat-tined digging fork is easier to use than a spade. Bastard-trench new ground being prepared for planting, also soil which has a hard pan or impervious layer at about spade depth. Clay soil should be left rough for the clods to weather. Light sandy soils usually only need turning over one spit deep. Breaking up the chalk underneath the top layer of soil on chalky soils is of long-term benefit. Soils kept in good heart by regular cultivation need less disturbance in depth.

Incorporate humus-forming organic materials into the soil. Almost any animal and plant waste can be used. As it decomposes it integrates with the mineral particles of soils, binding them into crumb or granular structure, with benefit to aeration and moisture retention and drainage (the soil should be able to retain moisture without becoming waterlogged). It becomes a base for bacterial and chemical activity, and a source and reserve of plant nutrients. Valuable sources are:

Manures. The so-called 'wet' manures – cow, farmyard, and pig – are traditionally favoured for sandy and light soils; the 'dry' manures – horse and sheep – for heavy soils, but all animal manures are good sources of humus, and small percentages of plant nutrients. Poultry (and pigeon) manure is an adequate alternative. A mixture of bedding materials (straw, bracken, peat, sawdust, wood shavings) increases humus content. When fresh and unrotted, use in autumn or early winter by spreading on vacant ground to allow for decomposition before incorporating it into the soil in the following growing season. Also available in pleasant to use dehydrated, compact forms.

Compost. This is a variable mixture of garden plant, and household organic wastes, pre-rotted for use at any time (see July notes). It makes an adequate humus substitute for manures when properly made.

Pulverised bark. The shredded and broken bark of trees, preferably partially composted, is a somewhat longer-lasting alternative to peat; it is best used in autumn and winter as an organic manure.

Peat. The sterile, partially decomposed remains of bog or moor plants, usually prepared and graded for garden use, are sedge peat or sphagnum moss peat. The former is slightly less acid than the latter. They make adequate humus manures, but are not rich in plant nutrients; may be used at any season, preferably moist in the warmer months and on light soils.

Seaweeds are well worth collecting for adding directly to soils, especially coastal sands, in autumn–winter. Comparatively rich in potash, they decompose quickly and are somewhat lacking in fibre.

Spent mushroom compost traditionally consists of well-rotted wheat-straw-based horse manure, mixed with a little soil, gypsum and lime, and is excellent for use as a humus manure in gardens, except for lime-intolerant plants.

☐ Other humus manures, which may be available only in limited or local supplies, such as spent hops from breweries, dried sewage and municipal composts from some local authorities, and shoddy, waste from woollen mills, are well worth using as autumn/winter manures.

Making leaf mould and compost
Rake up fallen leaves for making leaf mould or compost. If numerous enough, reserve beech, sweet chestnut, hornbeam and oak leaves for leaf mould. Stack them in a moist condition inside a netting enclosure, and allow to rot for 12–18 months, until the leaves break readily into tiny fragments. Although the leaves need to be moist, they need cover from soaking rains; a fall of snow is not harmful. A mixture of various leaves can be added to a general compost heap, or composted together with an activator (see July notes). All make humus-forming organic matter when rotted. Those with woody stalks and veins, such as

chestnut and sycamore may rot more slowly, however, and undecomposed parts can be returned to a fresh compost heap. Pine needles and coniferous foliage may take 2 or more years to rot and are best composted separately; they make good compost for raspberry and strawberry beds.

THE FLOWER GARDEN

Finish cutting down the last of the border Michaelmas daisies, golden rods etc. and use their stems and similar toughish growths of border plants chopped up at the base of a new compost heap.

Plant tulips early this month, 7.5–10cm (3–4in.) deep, in groups 10–15cm (4–6in.) apart, unless being used for formal bedding. Rub off the outer skins or tunics to check for greenish or greyish mould. Cut this out if present, and dust the bulb with a thiram fungicide before planting; reject badly affected bulbs. Mix a dressing of a calcified seaweed soil conditioner with clay soil before planting, or add coarse sand to the planting hole.

☐ Autumn-clean the herbaceous border. After cutting down the plant stems and removing the stakes, fork in a slow-acting fertiliser between the plants: use a dressing of bone meal and hoof and horn meal in equal parts by weight, with half a part of sulphate of potash, at 125g/m² (4oz per sq. yd) and top with an inch or so of sawdust, peat or forestry bark.

Gather tough woody waste materials, rose prunings, rose suckers, old raspberry, bramble and loganberry canes, fungi-infected dead wood, and diseased remains of plants for the bonfire, and light in a spell of calm, still weather. Keep the ash dry for use as a potash fertiliser in winter or spring; remember it also contains calcium (lime), which is good for most plants but not the lime-intolerant.

Cover Christmas roses (*Helleborus niger*), showing buds at the end of the month, with cloches so that the flowers can open pristine, unmarked by soil splashes.

THE VEGETABLE GARDEN

Prepare vacant ground for next year's crops, by digging, forking, ploughing or rotavating, to expose it to weathering, and give it time to re-consolidate before needed for sowing or planting. Double-dig or bastard-trench new ground or heavy ground that has not been dug deeply for a few years.

☐ Work in an organic manure for all crops except roots. Strew the material on the surface and turn it in as you cultivate, or place it loosely down the bottom of the digging trench and turn the soil over on to it. Do not bury too deeply.

'Clay' light soils, especially sands, which dry out too quickly in warm weather, by strewing sticky clods of clay over it, and leaving them until shattered by frost. They can then be dispersed evenly and forked in. This gives 'body' to the soil and is effective for some years.

Dress a heavy, sticky clay soil with horticultural gypsum before attempting to work it. Rake the gypsum with a scarifier or fork into the top few inches; it acts in a few weeks.

☐ Make mild-weather sowings this month or next of broad beans ('Aquadulce' or 'Aquadulce Claudia') only on sheltered and well-sunned sites in mild localities. In other areas, wait until February.

Cover the crowns of globe artichokes thickly with bracken, straw, leaves or litter, to protect them from frost.

☐ Stamp out club root in brassica crops by:
(a) removing and burning infected plants;
(b) liming the soil to bring to neutral (pH 7.0);
(c) improving drainage of the site;
(d) watering the soil with a 2 per cent solution of phenolic (Bray's) emulsion at 16 litres/m² (4 gall. per sq. yd).
Use the ground for a crop of beans, peas, potatoes or some other vegetable next year, then try brassicas again.

☐ Lift horse-radish roots for winter use, storing them in moist sand, in a shed, until wanted. Replant finger-thick thongs or roots where the invasive plant cannot become a nuisance.

☐ Lift ageing rhubarb plants, cut out the old centre, and replant pieces with robust healthy buds in humus-enriched, rather acid soil. Leave a few healthy pieces out on the surface to be frosted, and then take them into the greenhouse for forcing immediately the thaw comes.

Harvest turnips and swedes for storing in a cool shed or cellar, covered with sacking or straw.

THE FRUIT GARDEN

Planting
Now that the leaves have fallen, this is the ideal time for planting, although the season lasts until March.

Fruit trees: apples, pears and stone fruits. See that the trees are budded or grafted on to rootstocks chosen for the type of tree to be grown, and the kind of soil available. Cordon, espalier-trained and dwarf bush apples for good rich soils are best on E.M. (East Malling) IX dwarfing rootstocks; on poorish soils E.M. VII or M.M. (Malling-Merton) 106 semi-dwarfing rootstocks are likely to be better. Strong bush, half-standard or standard apples may be on M.M. 104 or M.M. 111 fairly vigorous rootstocks, and large standards for specimen or orchard planting on E.M. XXV rootstock. Cordon, espalier and bush pear trees are best on the Malling Quince A rootstock; standard trees are less suitable for gardens as they take many years to come into bearing. There are no reliable dwarfing rootstocks for plums and damsons, and bush, fan-trained, half-standard and standard trees are grafted on Brompton, Common Plum, and St Julien A rootstocks, as the most suitable.

☐ Prepare planting stations as follows:
(a) remove the topsoil one spit deep, placing it on plastic or hessian sheeting;
(b) break up the exposed lower soil, and enrich it with compost or rotted manure;
(c) Finish the base slightly convex or mounded, so that the roots can spread down and outward;
(d) add rotted manure, compost, moist peat or forestry bark to the topsoil liberally, at least one-third by bulk, with a handful of bone meal; do not use artificial fertilisers;
(e) place the tree on the mound (some growers like to put a slate or flat stone under the centre), so that it is planted at the same depth as it was grown in the nursery as shown by soil marks on the stem;
(f) insert a stake for bush and pyramid trees on dwarfing stocks;
(g) cover roots with the topsoil, firming it to the roots, and then fill the hole completely, treading the soil down with the heels; water if dry.
Plant cordon and trained-espalier trees against support wires on posts, and tie them in after settling in.

☐ Choose varieties to suit latitude and locality. Avoid 'Cox's Orange Pippin' north of the midlands; choose hardy plums and damsons rather than greengages in areas subject to hard frosts; do not plant early-flowering cherries and stone fruits on low-lying ground and acid soils. Make sure of reliable cropping by planting cross-pollinating varieties, as few fruit trees are completely self-fertile. Exceptions are morello cherry, Victoria plum and conference pear, but all do better in company. Consult a local grower or nurseryman before making a final selection.

Peach. Plant bush peach trees, grown on peach rootstocks or Brompton stocks in areas where they can be assured ample sun, well-drained soil containing some lime, and mild winters. In other areas, they are best grown on sunny warm walls.

Figs. Plant figs on a wall with a warm southerly aspect, with their roots severely restricted, early this month. Make a planting station by removing soil to a depth of about 75cm (2ft 6in.) in an area 1 metre square (3 × 3ft). Firm 30cm (12in.) of broken rubble, bricks or stone in the base; make walls of brick, concrete blocks, or asbestos sheeting to just above ground level; fill with 23cm (9in.) of chopped turf and soil or soil mixed with fibrous peat or forestry bark, and 23cm (9in.) of loam or topsoil, mixed with half as much shingle, small broken stone or coarse grit. Plant the tree in this, training shoots to the wall in a fan. 'Brunswick' and 'Brown Turkey' are good varieties.

Black currants. Plant on their own, or near culinary varieties of apples, where both can receive the high nitrogenous feeding they need. Cut back all shoots to just above outward-facing buds within 2.5cm (1in.) of their base after planting, to develop low-branching, well-shaped bushes.

Prune black currant (left) and red currant bushes (right) immediately after planting

Red and white currants. Plant with gooseberries or dessert varieties of apples, as they need feeds high in potash. Then prune according to the shape of plant required. For bushes, cut the central main shoot almost to the base, and side shoots to buds within 5–7.5cm (2–3in.) of their base. To grow as cordons cut the main shoot back by about half, and side shoots to within a bud or two from their base.

Raspberry canes. Plant in soil generously enriched with any kind of humus-forming organic matter. Space them 45–60cm (18in.–2ft) apart, and cut the canes down to 10cm (4in.) from ground level. Only late varieties such as 'November Abundance' or 'Zeva' are likely to crop next year. Raspberries like acid soils and heavy mulching.

Cultivated blackberries ('Parsley-leaved', 'Merton Thornless', 'Cregon Thornless', 'Bedford Giant'); hybrid berries ('Himalaya', 'Boysenberry', 'Youngberry'), and loganberries (a Thornless sport is available). Plant in acid soils, to train on fences, walls or wires, spaced 2.5–3.5m (8–12ft) apart; cut the canes back in spring by a half to two-thirds to young healthy growth.

Blueberry and cranberry. Plant selected cultivated varieties and hybrids early in the month in lime-free (essential), heath, peat or bog soils. They are evergreen, need little pruning, and crop without trouble.

Mulberry (*Morus alba* for leaves to feed silkworm caterpillars; *Morus nigra* for sweet, deep red, blackberry-like summer fruit). Plant on deep, well-drained soil, and in a sunny, warm sheltered garden where it has room to make a wide-spreading, medium-sized tree. No pruning is necessary except for the removal of dead wood, as cut shoots bleed freely.

Medlar (*Mespilus germanica* 'Dutch', 'Nottingham' and 'Royal'). Plant now on any soil, giving an open sunny situation. This native species makes a curious tree, grafted on to pear stock. Large solitary white flowers in late spring are followed by large, fattish round, brown fruits, picked in November, and 'bletted' (allowed to ripen, soften and turn yellow before being used). They are epicurean eating, useful for jelly and preserves.

☐ Begin winter pruning when leaves have fallen. First, remove all dead wood, cut out cankers and dress the wounds with a neat fungicide or bitumen tree paint. Prune apples and pears to encourage a well-spaced framework of branches; cutting back main leading or extension shoots by about a third to a half their past season's growth, and lateral or side shoots according to their vigour, pruning thin, weak shoots more severely. Bear in mind that severe pruning provokes strong shoot or wood growth; light pruning encourages flower bud formation. Once a good branching framework is established, and fruiting has begun, little winter pruning should be needed. Leave stone fruits alone to be pruned when in leaf.

☐ Thin out old congested trees, removing criss-crossing and inward growing branches or shoots completely. Thin clustered fruiting spurs to 2 buds, or behead the main branches, prior to re-grafting in March.

☐ Winter wash apple, pear and stone fruits after pruning or before the end of December, with a tar oil emulsion. Work on a dry calm day, with the objectives of destroying overwintering eggs of aphids, and stages of pests such as apple sucker, scale insects, fruit moths, and winter moths, cleaning the bark of green algae, lichen and moss growth, and checking bacterial blight. Apply to wet all surfaces of the branches and stems thoroughly. Currants, gooseberries, stone fruits, and ornamental relatives such as almonds, flowering cherries, crabs, and peaches also benefit. Wear old clothes and protective garments to prevent spray falling on the skin, eyes and face.

THE ORNAMENTAL GARDEN

Hedges
Do not plant evergreen and coniferous hedges once the temperature falls to 1.6–5°C (35–40°F) at night. Postpone until March–April, otherwise the plants lose moisture more quickly than they can replace it, and fail to grow in spring.

☐ Plant deciduous hedges at any time from now to the end of March, when the weather is mild and the soil open and easily worked; waterlogged soil conditions rather than frost endanger them. Plant beech, *Fagus sylvatica*, for an economical hedge and windbreak, brown with retained leaves in winter, on light and well-drained soils, or hornbeam (*Carpinus betulus*) for a stiffer,

174

even hardier, hedge of similar character, on heavy soils and low-lying sites. Plant quickthorn (*Crataegus monogyna*) in doubled staggered rows for a rapid-growing hedge which calls for a low outlay to start with but much maintenance later on.

Lawns

Lay new lawns from turf between now and March, given suitable weather, good soil conditions and a prepared site with good drainage. With the advent of pre-determined grass mixtures sown on fabric 'carpets' there is no real reason to rely on natural sod turf, with its weed problems and limited range of grasses, and heavy transport costs.

☐ Drain lawns subject to waterlogging and flooding in winter. Small areas can be improved by making 10–15-cm (4–6-in.) round holes to a depth of 75–90cm (2ft 6in.–3ft), 2m (6ft 6in.) apart, with a post-hole auger. Fill them in with broken stone, rubble, clinker and ash to within 15–23cm (6–9in.) of the surface, topping with an inch of leaves or fibrous peat and then replacing the topsoil and turf. Each hole acts as a drainage sump.

The Rock Garden

Paint out the top growth of any persistent weed with a solution of a paraquat/diquat contact weedkiller on a dry day while the weather remains mild (or weed by hand). This kills annual weeds and severely checks perennial ones, allowing alpine plants to flourish unhindered in the spring.

☐ Now is the time to plan and make a new rock garden. Try for an open situation, avoiding exposure to draughts, or frosts on low-lying sites. Where possible, plan with the main face facing south with an east–west orientation in the north and Scotland; but with a more north to south line with western-facing main face in the warmer south, so that plants are not too exposed to scorching sun. Incorporate good drainage materials at the base.

☐ To make a scree in which to grow many of the fascinating dwarf and high altitude alpines: put a layer of stones at the base, cover with leaves or coarse fibrous foliage and stems (such as bracken), and then at least 15cm (6in.) of stone chippings, admixed with a good sprinkling of loam and leaf mould. Sink occasional rocks in the scree alongside which plants can nestle.

☐ To make a rock bed or pavement where a raised, terraced rock garden is impractical: first, harrow or work crushed stone, gravel or chippings into the top 7.5cm (3in.) of soil. Then sink into it flat stones, about 5cm (2in.) thick, leaving spaces between for the insertion of choice alpine plants which soon revel in the good drainage and cool root-runs provided under the stones.

Roses

New roses can be planted from this month up to the end of March, if the soil is well prepared and the weather mild. Early planting is advantageous to establishment, especially on light soils.

Enrich light soils and sands with a load or two of clay or heavy loam prior to planting. Use only well-rotted manure, compost, peat or similar materials to mix with the topsoil, and use no chemical fertilisers at planting-time. Bone meal is safe, so is hoof and horn meal and seaweed powder.

☐ Plant ramblers and climbing roses in prepared soil, with their roots placed at least 30cm (12in.) from the foot of fences or walls, spreadeagled outward in the soil. Shorten coarse woody roots if necessary. If plants have been out of the soil rather too long, soak the roots overnight, and coat them with mud by dipping into a cream-like slurry of topsoil and water before planting.

☐ Plant roses for hedges where the soil is good, and exposure equable. Vigorous cluster roses make colourful informal hedges: 'Frensham', 'Queen Elizabeth', 'Masquerade', 'Iceberg', and 'Joseph's Coat' are suitable. For tall hedges, the hybrid Penzance sweetbriars 'Amy Robsart', 'Lady Penzance', 'Lord Penzance' and 'Meg Merrilees', grow to 2m (6ft 6in.).

Shrubs

Plant deciduous shrubs throughout the month, and up to the end of March, given mild weather and suitable soil conditions. Light frosts can be ignored; simply lift the frozen crust to one side. The soil underneath is quite friable, but lift it out on to a sheet of plastic so that frozen soil is not buried with it when replaced. Plant in the same way as fruit trees, keeping the ultimate spread and height of shrubs in mind. Infill empty spaces temporarily with quick-growing shrubs which can be scrapped later, such as bushes of santolina, lavender, sage, perennial candytuft and hypericums that can be readily propagated from cuttings.

☐ Hardwood, leafless cuttings can also be taken of such shrubs as ceanothus, forsythia, flowering currant, kerria, weigela, philadelphus, lonicera and deutzia, 15–20cm (6–8in.) long, from shoots of this year's growth. Cut below a node or bud, and insert for half their length in good topsoil, well-firmed, in a sheltered border. Hardwood cuttings of evergreens such as *Olearia haastii*, privet, laurels, rosemary, *Senecio greyii*, and *Skimmia japonica* can also be taken and rooted out of doors in good soil, preferably where they will enjoy shelter from frost. The cuttings should be covered by cloches in exposed areas.

Trees
Plant deciduous trees this month and until the end of March, given mild weather and amenable soil. Give adequate space for ultimate development in spread and height. Plant as instructed above for fruit trees. Stake tall-growing specimens at planting time.

☐ Take hardwood cuttings of dormant shoots of the current year's growth, 15–23cm (6–9in.) long, cut below a node, from such species as London plane (*Platanus × acerifolia*), laburnum, mulberry, poplars (such as *Populus candicans, P. lasiocarpa. P. nigra, P. trichocarpa* and most hybrids) and willows (*Salix* species). Insert firmly for half their length in reasonably good porous soil in open ground.

Walls
Plant deciduous climbers this month or during mild conditions in winter up to the end of March: self-clingers include *Hydrangea petiolaris*, Virginia creepers (*Parthenocissus* species), and *Vitis inconstans* and varieties; amongst the twiners are honeysuckle (*Lonicera periclymenum* and varieties), the rampant Russian vine, *Polygonum baldschuanicum*, and tendril climbers such as deciduous clematis. Wistaria needs a sheltered sunny south or west wall; *W. sinensis* is the most vigorous and hardy; *W. floribunda* and its varieties, especially 'Macrobotrys', the most beautiful; and *W. venusta* has the largest flowers. All require training, pruning twice a year, and do best in deep loam soils. Plant their roots outspread and placed at least 30cm (12in.) from the base of the wall or fence.

□ Plant the tall-growing wall border shrubs from now to March. Those that can be trained to grow on walls include *Chaenomeles speciosa* and varieties, *Cotoneaster horizontalis*, *Escallonia* varieties, *Forsythia ovata*, *Kerria japonica* and *Viburnum × juddii*, all of which adapt to any aspect.

The Water Garden
Visit the pool daily to remove any debris likely to foul the water; break any ice very gently, as vibrations from heavy blows through the water can concuss fish.

THE GARDEN UNDER GLASS

Clean cold frames which are empty; repaint wooden ones and an external paint suitable for frames and greenhouses. Treat red cedar woodwork with a specially formulated preserver. Replace the soil in permanent solid-based frames used for early crops and saladings.

□ Make a point of clearing and then sterilising the cold greenhouse, especially if there has been any mildew or disease present. Fumigate against a carry-over of parasitic fungi and their spores by burning sulphur candles in a closed house; *or* spray to wet all interior surfaces with a suitable fungicidal solution, or a 2 per cent solution of cresylic acid. Sterilise border soils, if they are to be retained (see December notes).

□ Keep the atmosphere in the cool greenhouse dryish, with a minimum night temperature of 7°C (45°F). Water growing plants moderately, preferably before noon. Try and maintain some circulation of air in damp weather by opening ventilators a little in the forenoon or midday; at this time of year, a fan ventilator is very useful.

□ Start bringing in bulbs potted earlier in the autumn, after 6 weeks, or when shoots show 5cm (2in.) of growth. Bring them into subdued light at first, with temperatures of 10–13°C (50–55°F), until the shoots show green, and then move to warmer conditions or indoors for forcing.

□ Pot up young winter and spring-flowering shrubs intended for the cold or cool greenhouse, and plunge out of doors in the soil or moist peat in good shelter, to bring in for flowering when buds show.

☐ Pot hardy winter-flowering heaths (*Erica herbacea* syn *E carnea*, *E.* × *darleyensis*, *E. erigena* syn. *E. mediterranea*, and their varieties) for winter colour in a cold greenhouse. Varieties of *Camellia japonica* and *C.* × *williamsii* can be potted up for winter/spring flowering, along with plants of the so-called Indian azalea (*Rhododendron simsii*).

☐ Cut back autumn-flowering chrysanthemums hard as they go out of bloom, placing them nearer the light to encourage formation of sturdy shoots for cuttings later on.

☐ Prune grape vines as soon as the leaves have fallen and the fruit has been harvested. Cut back all lateral shoots to above the first strong bud from their base and bend the main rods or stems downward until new growth begins. Dress the border for winter with bone meal and well-rotted organic matter. New vines may be planted now, either in the soil borders of the greenhouse, or with their roots in good soil just outside it, the new rod being led into the greenhouse via a drain pipe or opening in the greenhouse wall.

☐ Clean up trained nectarines or peaches, remove fallen leaves and any moribund wood for burning. At the first sign of leaf curl, spray the trees with a benomyl fungicide. This is the time to plant new trees, in the border soil enriched with bone meal and well-rotted organic matter.

☐ Rhubarb roots and crowns that were exposed to frost earlier this month are now ready for forcing: box them up covered with loamy soil and bring them into the cool greenhouse. Leave them under the staging and water to keep moist.

December

Some December plants in flower and vegetables in season

The Flower Garden
Hyacinth
Iris unguicularis

The Ornamental Garden
Erica (heaths)
Hamamelis mollis
Jasminum nudiflorum (winter jasmine)
Mahonia
Chimonanthus (winter sweet)

Vegetables in season
Artichoke, Jerusalem
Brussels sprouts
Cabbage
Chicory
Leek
Swede

THE FLOWER GARDEN

Protect plants likely to flower this month or next: hellebores and *Iris unguicularis* usually bloom during the month (although the majority of the hellebores don't open until the new year) and need protection from slugs; provide cover unless, in the case of the iris, it is grown in a sunny, warm south-facing wall border. Ocassionally there is a surprise precocious flowering of primroses, epimediums, violas, pansies, and other early spring-blooming species in brief mild warm spells.

Prevent mice and voles from digging up crocus corms by pegging fine mesh plastic netting over them, and put down a repellent, especially at the entrance of small holes.

☐ If there is a spell of good planting weather, take the opportunity to make a special planting of border plants that appeal to you, suited to your soil and situation. Distinctive plants include the *Hosta* species and varieties, for varied foliage and cover in shade; red hot pokers, *Kniphofia* species, for a summer spectacle; *Astilbe* varieties for moist or boggy ground; a range of *Campanula* species on chalk; a cluster of day lilies, *Hemerocallis*, for summer in almost any soil; of sword-leaved New Zealand flax, *Phormiumtenax*, with colourful foliage for mild gardens; and the true *Geranium* in its several species and varieties, for dryish shade.

☐ Take root cuttings of herbaceous plants such as *Anchusa azurea*, *Echinops ritro*, *Papaver orientale* (oriental poppy), and *Romneya* now. Detach side roots of pencil- to finger-thickness, 5–10cm (2–4in.) long with a horizontal surface at the top and a sloping one at the bottom. Keep them in moist sand in a cool place until March or April; then insert upright as they grow on the plant, in boxes or pots of good compost and transfer to a cold frame, greenhouse or under cloches to grow on. Thin fibrous root cuttings should be started off laid flat in boxes of compost strewn over with sand.

Make a clean cut with a sharp knife when taking root cuttings

THE VEGETABLE GARDEN

Use every opportunity to complete digging and organic manuring before the turn of the year. Take advantage of frozen ground to get organic manure or compost distributed on it, ready to be incorporated as soon as the frost goes. Avoid walking on sticky clay soil after a thaw, or when it is wet enough to stick to your boots, as compressed clay dries out hard and solid.

☐ Firm the roots of brassica crops lifted by frost immediately, without waiting for the thaw.

Protect Brussels sprouts, broccoli, cauliflower, sprouting broccoli and spring cabbage from the attentions of wood pigeons and birds by stretching nets over them, high enough to prevent the birds weighing the nets down on the vegetables.

☐ Cover crowns of rhubarb with rotted manure, compost or leaf mould, and place a bottomless bucket, old chimney pot or box over them, partly filled with straw, to produce early pale pink tender stalks.

THE FRUIT GARDEN

Fruit trees and soft fruit. Complete winter pruning and application of a tar-oil wash to apples, pears, stone fruits and soft fruits before the end of the month. Any further delay must result in damage to buds.

☐ Keep the area under the branches of fruit trees clear of grass and weeds which compete with the trees' roots for moisture and nourishment. Clearing the ground will also improve soil aeration and penetration by rain, and facilitate manuring and feeding.

☐ Winter-feed trees and bushes with slow-acting fertilisers and manures. Provide phosphorus in the form of bone meal to all fruits, every second or third year. Provide nitrogen in hoof and horn meal (and organic manure or compost) annually, especially to black currants, culinary apples and pears. Provide a yearly feed of potash in sulphate of potash or powdered seaweed, especially to red and white currants, gooseberries, and dessert apples. Top fertiliser dressings with one of humus-forming organic material.

☐ Stop rabbits and hares from eating the bark of young trees, either by smearing the stems with fruit-tree banding grease as high as the animals can reach, or by fitting plastic guards round the stems. Damaged trees will recover provided the bark has not been removed all the way round the stems; but wounds should be pared clean of ragged bark, and dressed with a fungicidal tree dressing.

☐ Check over apples and pears in store, and remove promptly any that are going bad. A strong fruit odour is caused by ethylene gas from fruits ripening too quickly. It means that the store needs ventilating.

☐ Cut out and burn shoots carrying bands or rings of globular eggs, deposited by the lackey moth, which hatch into leaf-devouring caterpillars in spring.

☐ Outdoor vines should be planted before Christmas. They need a sunny wall, or an open sunny situation in a favourable climate where they may be grown in rows, trained on wires. The fruit needs a warm autumn to ripen, even though it is hardy. The 'Strawberry Grape' is a good first choice of fruit. 'Brandt', 'Madeleine Royale', 'Müller Thurgau', 'Royal Muscadine', and 'Seyve-Villard 5/276' are good for wine-making.

THE ORNAMENTAL GARDEN

Paths
Mark out and construct paths when weather permits. To be sure of dry footing in wet situations place a line of drain-pipes underneath, in a foundation layer of broken stone, bricks or rubble.

Lawns
Check for the presence of leather-jackets, the greyish brown larvae of the crane-fly (daddy-long-legs) when tufts of dying grass come away easily in the hand, and starlings are busy pecking and feeding. The grubs are found just under the turf. Treat them with a dressing of a carbaryl (sevin) or derris insecticidal dust bulked with sand, in a mild spell.

Test the soil for acidity (see February notes). If more than moderately acid (pH 6.2), give an application of ground limestone, or, on acid clay, basic slag.

Finish re-turfing on light soils by the end of the month to ensure a smooth look for summer.

Do not work on the lawn in frost or snow; do not even walk on it, as fine grasses may be bruised and damaged.

Roses

Carry on planting new roses in mild weather, into prepared soil (see November notes). If you want to plant shrub roses in shrub and flower borders, some successful and popular ones are *Rosa × alba* 'Amelia'; *R. gallica* 'Versicolor'; 'Golden Chersonese', *R. hugonis*; *R. centifolia* (moss rose) 'Muscosa', 'Blanche Moreau', 'Old Pink', and 'William Lobb'; *R. moschata* (musk rose) hybrids; *R. moyesii*; 'Nevada'; *R. rugosa* 'Alba', 'Blanc Double de Coubert', 'Frau Dagmar Hastrup', 'Roseraie de l'Hay, and 'Rubra'; *R. pimpinellifolia* (burnet rose); *R. p. altaica*, and *R. p. lutea*; *R. villosa* (apple rose) syn. *R. pomifera*; *R. webbiana*; *R. willmottiae*; *R. xanthina* and *R. × spontanea*. All have handsome foliage, robust growth, and often colourful fruits, and need little pruning or maintenance.

Shrubs

Top-dress lime-tolerant rhododendrons and ericas with oak leaf-mould if available; or with decaying woodland floor leaves and even rotten fragmented branches and wood, which is what they like naturally, or moist dark sphagnum moss peat. If the bushes are flowering poorly add a dressing of 1 part hoof and horn meal, 3 parts superphosphate, and 1 part sulphate of potash, at about 60g/m² (2oz per sq. yd) over the rooting area. Do not use lime or alkaline-reacting fertilisers such as bone meal and wood ash.

Trees

Prune and carry out surgery on deciduous trees such as ash, beech, birch, chestnut, elder, hornbeam, robinia, rowan, thorn, whitebeam and willow this month, if needed. Finish cuts flush at a junction with other branches or stems, leaving no snags to die back. Do not prune trees that may 'bleed' such as those of the *Prunus* genus (almonds, cherries, plums and so on), maples (*Acer* species) and walnuts, until they are in leaf.

☐ Be sure of berries on holly trees by planting male and female plants together, as they are unisexual, and only the females berry; such as *Ilex* × *altaclarensis* 'Golden King' (obviously misnamed) and 'Wilsonii'; and *I. aquifolium* 'Bacciflava' (yellow berries). Males are best chosen for their showy foliage: *I.* × *altaclarensis* 'Hodginsii', *I. a.* 'Golden Queen' and *I. a.* 'Silver Queen' are good choices.

☐ Tie bands of tape or twine around the branches of cypresses and upright-branching and growing conifers which might be broken under the weight of heavy snow.

☐ Some planting suggestions for beautiful winter specimen trees with distinctive bark: *Acer griseum, A. palmatum heptalobum* 'Senkaki', varieties of *Betula pendula* (silver birch), *Parrotia persica, Prunus serrula, Salix alba* 'Vitellina', or *Tilia platyphyllos.*

THE GARDEN UNDER GLASS

The Cool Greenhouse

Continue to keep an air-buoyant atmosphere, ventilating lightly in the midday hours, watering to keep soils just moist, and sparingly on cloudy or rainy days; maintain equable heat.

Liquid-feed plants in bud or coming into flower moderately, with diluted liquid manure, or seaweed extract.

Keep flowering annuals such as clarkia, godetia and schizanthus fairly close to the glass and source of light, to prevent them becoming drawn and spindly.

☐ Keep perpetual-flowering carnations, now in a flush of flowering, thriving with gentle watering to keep the soil moist, and a night temperature of 7°C (45°F), rising to 13–15.5°C (55–60°F) during the day. Water early in the day; cover soil around plants with a thin layer of limestone chippings to avoid collar rot from water lodging at the base.

☐ Keep winter-flowering begonias healthy with sufficient ventilation to maintain a change of air daily, light watering, varied with a weekly feed of diluted liquid manure or fertiliser, and a night temperature of at least 10°C (50°F).

☐ Take cuttings of sturdy shoots of Japanese chrysanthemums, regal pelargoniums and carnations, as and when available, rooting in pots in a porous compost with a little bottom heat of 15.5°C (60°F).

☐ If you can get good loam or first-class topsoil for use in John Innes seed and potting composts, sterilise it by heat or chemical treatment. Heat the soil through to 82°C (180°F) for 10 minutes, preferably by using one of the simple electrical sterilisers on the market according to the makers' instructions. This destroys all parasitic fungi, insects, viruses and weed seeds without impairing the soil. Cool before use. A small-scale method is to place 1cm (½in.) water in a large saucepan and bring it to the boil; sift in air-dry soil to fill; boil up again for 20 minutes; tip out the wet soil on to a clean surface to lose surplus moisture. When cool, it is ready for use.

☐ Many house plants can be grown under cool greenhouse conditions, and moved to the house when at their best. Cool means temperatures of 7–10°C (45–50°F) at night, rising to 13–15.5°C (55–60°F) by day. Suitable subjects for this treatment include such plants as gently forced flowering bulbs in pots and bowls, indoor azaleas (*Rhododendron simsii*), *Cyclamen persicum*, *Primula malacoides*, *P. obconica*, *P. sinensis* and their varieties, fibrous rooted begonias and cineraria. To them can be added foliage plants such as *Cissus antartica*, *Ficus elastica*, *Hedera helix* in its variegated foliage forms, *Philodendron scandens*, *Sansevieria trifasciata* 'Laurentii', *Aspidistra elatior*, *Schlumbergera truncata*, *Tradescantia fluminensis* and *Zebrina pendula*. Their needs are simple: good light without direct hot sun, freedom from draughts, open, porous compost, no over-watering, and moderate humidity – assured in dry indoor atmospheres by placing their containers on pebble-filled saucers which are kept moist.

Index

Page numbers in bold type refer to illustrations.